Bi

Alexander Pushkin

Brief Lives:
Alexander Pushkin

Robert Chandler

*With translations of his poetry
by Robert Chandler, Stanley Mitchell
and Antony Wood*

ET REMOTISSIMA PROPE

Brief Lives
Published by Hesperus Press Limited
4 Rickett Street, London sw6 1RU
www.hesperuspress.com

First published by Hesperus Press Limited, 2009

Designed and typeset by Fraser Muggeridge studio
Printed in Jordan by Al-Khayyam Printing Press

ISBN: 978-1-84391-912-4

Contents

Childhood and ancestry
1799–1811

When Pushkin was one year old, his nurse once took him out to the park. Suddenly coming across Tsar Paul, she did not have time to remove Pushkin's little cap. The sovereign went up to her, scolded her for her slowness and removed the child's cap himself. In later life Pushkin was to say that his dealings with the Court went back all the way to the days of Tsar Paul.

P.V. Annenkov, 1855

Alexander Pushkin was born in Moscow on 26th May (6th June New Style) 1799,[1] and he was to remain in Moscow throughout his childhood. He had an elder sister, Olga, and a younger brother, Lev. Five more siblings were born after Lev, but they all died in infancy.

Pushkin's mother, Nadezhda Osipovna, was known as 'the beautiful Creole'; one of her grandfathers was a black African. She was domineering and restless; between 1801 and 1811 the family moved from one lodging to another eleven times. If a change of lodging was impossible, she would move the furniture or change the wallpaper. She seems to have been distant, even cruel, in her treatment of Alexander – perhaps because he looked like her half-black father, with whom she got on badly; she made it clear that she preferred both Olga and Lev. The lack of contact between Pushkin and his parents was unusual even by the standards that prevailed among the upper classes of the time.

Pushkin's father, Sergei Lvovich, seems to have been frivolous, irritable, and dominated by his wife. Little seems to have mattered to him apart from his social life. He was incompetent in his management of the family estate; both he and his wife were only too ready to live beyond their means.

If Pushkin's parents were important to his development mainly through their emotional absence, there were other relatives who played a more positive role. His father's brother, Vasily Lvovich, was a competent poet himself; he was fond of Pushkin and aware of his brilliance. He knew most of the important writers of the time, including the historian Nikolai Karamzin and the poets Batyushkov, Dmitriev and Zhukovsky – and most of these writers visited Pushkin's home. Pushkin was evidently brought up in an atmosphere that encouraged him to read and write poetry.

By the age of ten, according to his sister, Pushkin had read Plutarch, the *Iliad* and the *Odyssey* in French, and much of the eighteenth-century French literature in his father's library. In other respects, however, he was a poor student, and he seems to have failed, even as an adult, to master basic arithmetic.

Still more important than Vasily Lvovich was Pushkin's maternal grandmother, Maria Gannibal. She lived with the family from 1805 and was responsible for the running of the house and the education of the children; it was she who engaged their various French tutors and governesses. Apart from the household serfs, she was the only person with whom Pushkin spoke Russian at home; with the rest of the family he spoke French. She was fond of Pushkin, but she would sometimes tell her friends that she had no idea what would become of him, saying that her elder grandson was a bad student and that he rarely prepared his lessons properly.

Maria Gannibal also helped to instil in Pushkin a sense of family history that was to remain with him throughout his life.

It is possible that the inadequacy of his parents made it all the more vital to him to feel a connection to the generations before them.

The Pushkins belonged to the old Russian nobility. They had never occupied the very highest positions in the Russian state, but in the sixteenth and seventeenth centuries several Pushkins had played roles of historical significance; Pushkin includes two of them in his historical drama *Boris Godunov*. Pushkin took pleasure in the knowledge that several of his ancestors were rebels; he refers several times in his works to Fyodor Pushkin, who was executed for taking part in a rebellion against Peter the Great in 1697 – 'for refusing to yield over a matter of conscience', as Pushkin himself puts it. Pushkin also refers at least twice to his paternal grandfather, Lev Alexandrovich, who lost all chance of promotion at court by remaining loyal to Peter III even after the latter was overthrown by his wife – the empress we now know as Catherine the Great.

Important as earlier Pushkins were to him, not one of them was as important to his imagination as his maternal great-grandfather, Abram Gannibal. Gannibal's story is unusual, and some elements of it remain controversial. He was born in 1696; it now seems likely that he came not from Ethiopia, as was long believed, but from Chad. As a boy, he was taken by Islamic slave-traders to Constantinople. From there he was taken to Moscow – perhaps at the instigation of Peter the Great, who was always interested in anyone or anything exotic. There were, at this time, Negro servants in many of the main European courts. When Abram arrived in Moscow at the age of eight, Peter became his godfather and took responsibility for his education.

Gannibal proved equally gifted in languages, maths and science. As a young man, he became Peter's most trusted aide. Sent by Peter to study in France, he was befriended by Diderot and Voltaire, who referred to him as the 'dark star of Russia's enlightenment'. Fifty years later, when Diderot needed money,

Gannibal would persuade Catherine the Great to buy his library and pay him a pension.

On his return from France, Gannibal was appointed 'principal translator of foreign books at the Imperial Court'. But he not only translated books about scientific and military matters; he was also an uncommonly gifted engineer himself. By 1759 he had been promoted to the rank of general and was in charge of military engineering throughout Russia. One of the forts he constructed – Kronstadt in the Gulf of Finland – was still of military importance 200 years later, during the Siege of Leningrad. Gannibal was awarded several estates, and he was granted the status of a hereditary nobleman.

The death of the Empress Elizabeth in 1761 put an end to his career, and he spent his last twenty years on his Mikhailovskoye estate, near Pskov. There, in Pushkin's words, 'the black African who had become a Russian noble lived out his life like a French *philosophe.*'

To the end of his life, Pushkin treasured a gift, from his friend Pavel Nashchokin, of an inkwell with a statuette of a black man leaning against an anchor in front of two bales of cotton. Pushkin refers to Gannibal many times in his work, and in 1827 he began a novel about him: *The Blackamoor of Peter the Great.* Pushkin's own physical appearance was unusual for a Russian; with his swarthy complexion and his dark, curly hair, he was generally seen as exotic. It seems likely that, in the following passage from *The Blackamoor of Peter the Great*, Pushkin is also describing himself:

Usually people looked at the young blackamoor as if he were a marvel, clustering around him and showering him with greetings and questions, and this curiosity, though seemingly well-intentioned, wounded his self esteem. The sweet attentions of women, almost the only goal of our efforts, not only failed to gladden his heart but even filled it with bitterness and indignation. He felt that they saw him as some kind of rare beast, a kind of special, alien creation that had been accidentally transported into a world that had nothing to do with him.

Andrey Sinyavsky, in *Strolls with Pushkin* (a high-spirited book that Sinyavsky composed in the late 1960s, in a Soviet labour camp, and sent out in instalments in letters to his wife), has written that Pushkin 'seized on his Negroid appearance and his African past, which he loved perhaps more dearly than he did his aristocratic (Russian) ancestry'. This points to an important paradox. Pushkin saw himself as an outsider and defiantly identified with someone he saw as still more of an outsider. Gannibal, however, was not only an outsider; he was also very close to no less a man than Peter the Great – and in *The Blackamoor* Pushkin chose to exaggerate this closeness. Pushkin's identification with Gannibal was also a way of making himself into an insider, an intimate of Russia's greatest Tsar; it may have helped him to write more freely about Peter – and about Russian history in general.

The Imperial Lycée
1811–17

My friends, this brotherhood of ours will live.
United, like the soul, it cannot perish.
Secure and free to prosper, it will flourish
On sustenance the friendly Muses give.

Pushkin, '19 October', 1825, tr. Henry Jones

On 19th October 1811, aged twelve, Pushkin began his studies at
the prestigious Imperial Lyceum; he was part of the first intake
of thirty students.

The Lycée, as it was usually known, was a remarkable institution – the most progressive of its day. It was housed in a wing
of the Great Palace at Tsarskoye Selo, the summer residence,
sixteen miles from St Petersburg, of the imperial family; its ethos
was liberal, and it enjoyed extraordinary privileges. Its purpose,
according to an imperial decree, was 'the education of the young,
especially those destined for important parts of government service'. Corporal punishment was forbidden. Teachers were never
to allow pupils 'to use words without clear ideas', and they were
to encourage 'the exercise of reason' in all subjects. Teaching
was mostly carried out in Russian – not, as was then common, in
French. Each student had his own small study-bedroom. The one
strangely harsh regulation was that the boys were not allowed
to leave the Lycée throughout the six years of their studies. Even
the July vacation had to be spent at the school, and parents

and relatives were allowed to visit only on Sundays or other holidays.

In July 1811, on the suggestion of Alexander Turgenev (a friend of the family and an important historian, not to be confused with the well-known novelist Ivan Turgenev), Pushkin had been sent by his parents to take the oral entrance examination. This was conducted by the Minister of Education, the Lycée's first director Vasily Malinovsky, and one other official. Pushkin was accepted, though Malinovsky's private note read, 'Flighty and frivolous. Excellent at French and drawing, lazy and backward at arithmetic.' Except in his best subjects – Russian and French literature and fencing – Pushkin did not prove a good student, and Malinovsky's assessment is echoed in later reports. One written in November 1812 reads:

> His talents are brilliant rather than fundamental, his mind more ardent and subtle than deep. His application to study is moderate [...] Having read a great number of French books, often inappropriate to his age, he has filled his memory with many successful passages of famous authors; he is also reasonably well read in Russian literature, and knows many fables and light verses. His knowledge is generally superficial...

The Lycée was ceremonially opened on 19th October 1811, in the presence of Tsar Alexander I, to whom the pupils were introduced individually. On the whole, the school seems to have run smoothly. There are mentions in memoirs of the mischievous behaviour of the boys, but there was only one case of expulsion during the six years Pushkin spent there. The Russian critic, D.S. Mirsky, describes the curriculum as giving a general groundwork in the humanities and modern culture but 'being calculated rather to develop an easy-going conversationalist and man of the world than either a serious scholar or an efficient statesman'. One tutor, Alexander Kunitsyn, had a lasting influence on Pushkin; the imprint of his thoughts about freedom, natural law and the relation between the individual and society can be seen in Pushkin's mature work.

More important to Pushkin than any of the tutors were his fellow students. The members of the Lycée's first intake formed a close fellowship. They referred to themselves as 'a nation', and they held a reunion every year for the rest of their lives on 19th October, the anniversary of the Lycée's opening. Pushkin was in exile from 1820 to 1826, but he attended four times during the next ten years; and in 1825, 1827, 1831 and 1836 he wrote poems dedicated to the occasion. For Pushkin, 19th October was a date intimately bound up with reflections on his own fate, the fate of his contemporaries and the fate of Russia. The 'publisher's note' accompanying the original, anonymous publication of *The Captain's Daughter* was dated 19th October 1836 – almost as if this were the equivalent of his signature. And it was on 19th October 1830 that Pushkin burned the unfinished 'Decembrist' chapter of *Eugene Onegin*.

The lasting closeness that developed among the members of the Lycée's first intake is remarkable. There is no doubt that the Lycée was sensitively and generously run, but there may have been other determinants. The decade following the defeat of Napoleon was a brief golden age for St Petersburg. Russia had, at last, become a major European power. There seemed no reason to doubt that the westernising project begun by Peter the Great would continue, but Russian writers no longer felt that they need remain forever in the shadow of French, German and English writers. The Imperial Lycée, western-orientated in many ways but with Russian as its main language of instruction, seemed destined to play a crucial role in this new Russia, and the boys who formed its first intake may well have felt chosen by fate. As Mirsky remarks:

… in this feeling of Pushkin's towards his school, compared to his attitude towards his home and family, there is a symbolical significance: all Petrine Russia belonged more to its school than to its home. Its school was Europe and Civilisation, its home the old traditional Russia.

No less remarkable was the amount of poetic talent to be found in this first intake. Pushkin's two closest friends were Ivan Pushchin, who later became a magistrate, and the poet Anton Delvig. His other friends included Wilhelm Küchelbecker, an intelligent critic and an interesting, unusual poet; Illichevsky, who wrote elegant epigrams; and Mikhail Yakovlev, a composer who set a number of Pushkin's and Delvig's poems to music. Both Pushkin and Delvig were soon publishing in the main literary magazines of the day. A poem dedicated to Küchelbecker and signed by an anagram of Pushkin's name was published in the prestigious *The Messenger of Europe* when Pushkin was only fifteen years old.

Pushkin wrote a great deal while at the Lycée: bawdy epigrams, conventional love poems, patriotic reflections, light verse. Nearly all of his verse from these years is elegant; none of it is great poetry. It is all the more impressive that Pushkin's seniors were so quick, and so generous, in their recognition of his talent.

In 1815, Gavrila Derzhavin, the greatest Russian poet of the age of Catherine the Great, heard Pushkin recite his poem 'Recollections at Tsarskoye Selo' at a public examination at the Lycée. Derzhavin, who had until then been half asleep, was enthralled; he is said to have told a friend that Pushkin had already outshone all other writers. Derzhavin was by then already seventy-one years old – an age by which most writers have long since lost the ability to appreciate the talents of the young. Pushkin later memorialised the occasion:

And with a smile my Muse was greeted;
Our first success emboldened us,
We were by old Derzhavin heeded
And blessed before he joined the dust...
Eugene Onegin, VIII, 2

Several other leading poets – Prince Pyotr Vyazemsky, Konstantin Batyushkov and Vasily Zhukovsky – expressed similar enthusiasm. In a letter to Vyazemsky, Zhukovsky wrote, 'He is the hope of our literature. I fear only lest he, imagining himself mature, should prevent himself from becoming so. We must all unite to assist this future giant, who will outgrow us all, to grow up.' And on one occasion Karamzin recommended Pushkin to a minor poet, Prince Neledinsky-Meletsky, who found himself unable to compose the poem he had promised for the farewell party of the Grand Duchess Anna. Having just married, she was about to leave for Holland with her husband, Prince William of Orange. Pushkin quickly produced some appropriate verses, and these were sung at the supper in the gardens of the Pavlovsk palace; the dowager empress rewarded him with the gift of a gold watch and chain.

A great poet seldom, if ever, appears out of nowhere. Shakespeare was heir to the earlier Elizabethan poets, playwrights and translators of Ovid. Dante was heir to the Provençal tradition and the *dolce stil nuovo* developed by Guido Guinizzelli and Guido Cavalcanti. Similarly, Karamzin, Batyushkov and Zhukovsky had prepared the ground for Pushkin; they also had literary battles to fight and were probably glad of a talented young recruit.

As a literary language, Russian is very young. From the middle ages until the reign of Peter the Great, the written language of the Russian state was Church Slavonic – a language that is closer to Bulgarian than to Russian and the status of which was much like that of Latin in medieval western Europe. It was only gradually, in the course of the eighteenth century, that literary Russian took shape – an initially awkward blend of spoken Russian and Church Slavonic, with poorly digested borrowings from the languages of western Europe.

While Pushkin was studying at the Lycée, two different camps of writers were fighting to determine the shape of literary Russian. 'The Colloquy of Lovers of the Russian Word', headed by Admiral Shishkov, stood for an archaic Russian studded with Church Slavonicisms. The new school, headed by Karamzin, stood for a more modern, flexible language, incorporating borrowings from French but at the same time closer to ordinary spoken Russian. In 1815 the new school founded *Arzamas*, a literary-cum-dining society named after a small town famous for its geese. They met regularly until spring 1818 and seem to have spent most of their time laughing at the Shishkovians. As well as writing parodies, they staged mock rituals – sometimes mock burials of their older rivals. Pushkin was still at the Lycée and so unable to attend, but he was, nevertheless, accepted as a member – a considerable honour for a sixteen-year-old. He was nicknamed 'the cricket' because of his quick wit and general liveliness (at the Lycée he was known as 'the monkey' – because of his physical appearance – and 'the Frenchman' – because of his knowledge of French literature and also, probably, because of his enjoyment of sexual jokes). *Arzamas* was not a long-lived society, but his association with it proved important to Pushkin. Through it, he developed lasting friendships and alliances with older writers. Zhukovsky, Vyazemsky and Alexander Turgenev were to prove loyal protectors throughout Pushkin's life and even after his death.

St Petersburg
1817–20

Applause all round. Onegin enters,
Treading on toes at every stall;
Askew, his double eyeglass centres
On ladies whom he can't recall.

Eugene Onegin, I, 21

The decade between the defeat of Napoleon and the Decembrist rebellion in 1825 was a heady time to be a young aristocrat in St Petersburg. Pushkin threw himself with abandon into all the entertainments the city offered. As a graduate of the Lycée, he was bound to enter public service; he was attached to the Foreign Ministry, but his appointment was entirely nominal.

Pushkin's family had moved to St Petersburg in 1814, and he joined them in their chaotic apartment in the unfashionable Kolomna district. There he was also reunited with Nikita Kozlov, a serf from his father's estate who had looked after him as a child and who now became his valet. Nikita had married the daughter of Arina Rodionovna, who had been a nurse to all three Pushkin children, and he was to remain with Pushkin until his death.

St Petersburg has often seemed to be not so much a working city as a giant theatre. Peter the Great had founded the city in uninhabited marshland, used all his powers of coercion to create a capital of grandiose beauty, and then compelled the Russian aristocracy to play – on this stage-set he had created – at being

Europeans. It was not by chance that the most important institution in the life of the aristocracy, other than the court itself, was the theatre. Several of the nobility had their own theatres, there was a theatre in the Winter Palace, and the public Bolshoy Theatre had reopened in 1818 with a stage that could accommodate several hundred performers. Pushkin adored the theatre, went to countless performances and pursued many of the actresses and ballerinas; all of this is reflected in the first chapter of *Eugene Onegin*.

In March 1819, Nikita Vsevolozhsky, a wealthy young man, set up a small private society known as *The Green Lamp*. Pushkin and his friend Delvig were both members. Meetings were fortnightly; the young men gambled, drank champagne, talked radical politics and read aloud poems and theatre reviews that they had written. The atmosphere of frivolity and generous high spirits is well captured in a story about Pushkin's manuscripts. In 1820, playing against Vsevolozhsky, Pushkin staked – and lost – a collection of manuscripts of his early poems that the two of them had valued at 1,000 roubles; his government salary (his only regular income at the time) was 700 roubles a year. Four years later, wanting to publish these poems, Pushkin asked his brother Lev to buy back the manuscript. Vsevolozhsky asked for only 500 roubles but Pushkin, even though he was in constant debt, insisted on paying the full amount. *The Green Lamp* was not as important to Pushkin as *Arzamas*, but its members were his own age and shared his tastes. Pushkin's *Arzamas* friends, in contrast, were older than he was and tended to disapprove of what they saw as his dissipated way of life.

Pushkin's need for women seems to have been unusually intense. A fellow student at the Lycée wrote, 'Pushkin was so fond of women that, at the age of just fifteen or sixteen, his eyes would catch fire, at a Lycée ball, just from touching the hand of his dancing partner. He would snort and blow, like a spirited stallion in a young herd.' His relationships with women varied from the most casual to the most intense, and from the platonic to the purely sensual. He visited prostitutes, chased after unattainable beauties, and fell in love, often with older women. Sometimes he treated women casually, but more often he was in love. Women found him attractive, even though no one thought him good-looking. He described himself as an 'ugly descendant of negroes'. He was short, and he had pale blue eyes. His curly black hair was often dishevelled, and he prided himself on his long fingernails. His most striking characteristic seems to have been his extreme restlessness.

He suffered several severe illnesses during these years – both fevers and bouts of venereal disease. These illnesses may have been necessary to him; it was when he was ill that he did much of his writing. In December 1818 Alexander Turgenev wrote to Vyazemsky, 'for all the dissoluteness of his life, [Pushkin] is finishing the fourth canto of his poem. Two or three more doses of clap – and it'll be in the bag.'

Another important element in the life of Pushkin and his contemporaries was duelling. Like his love affairs, Pushkin's duels seem to have been of every possible degree of seriousness. On one occasion, Küchelbecker took offence at a jokey poem of Pushkin's and challenged him. Delvig was Küchelbecker's second. Pushkin's recent English biographer T.J. Binyon recounts what happened next:

> Küchelbecker was to have the first shot. When he began to aim, Pushkin shouted: 'Delvig! Stand where I am, it's safer here.' Incensed, Küchelbecker made a half-turn, his pistol went off and blew a hole in Delvig's hat. Pushkin refused to fire, and the quarrel was made up.[2]

Other duels, in contrast, were in deadly earnest. Pushkin acquired a reputation for irascibility and bravado, and he may have been lucky to survive these duels unscathed.

The poem that Turgenev described as having been helped along by a bout of clap was *Ruslan and Lyudmila*, a narrative poem of nearly 3,000 lines. Pushkin's first book, it was published in July 1820 – by which date Pushkin was already in exile. Its grace, humour and fluency brought it great popularity. Mirsky describes it as 'akin to the poetry of the classical ballet […] it is a romance, but the romantic element is seen through a prism of eighteenth-century frivolity.' It begins with the wedding of Lyudmila, daughter of Prince Vladimir of Kiev, to Ruslan. The couple are about to make love when Lyudmila is carried away by the wizard Chernomor. After many adventures, Ruslan defeats Chernomor, sees off other rivals, routs an army that was besieging Kiev and returns in triumph with Lyudmila.

Like his duels and his affairs with women, Pushkin's poetry assumed many forms: jokey 'letters' addressed to friends, erotic poems, poems of romantic love, sharp epigrams aimed at the Tsar and his ministers. His political poems circulated widely in manuscript. 'Liberty: an Ode' (1817) ends with the lines:

> So understand from now, O Tsars,
> That neither punishment nor rewards,
> Neither base dungeons nor high altars
> Can ever truly serve as guards.
> Be first, O Tsars, to bow your heads
> Beneath the faithful shade of Law –
> May Peace and Freedom be your guards
> Beside your throne for evermore!

This conclusion is, in fact, moderate and liberal, but the authorities and the radicals alike saw the poem as revolutionary – perhaps because of a reference in it to the murder in 1801 of Tsar Paul I.

The political climate was quickly becoming more dangerous. The Napoleonic Wars had engendered, particularly among the elite, a desire for greater freedom. Young officers who had fought in Germany or served in the Russian forces occupying part of northeastern France from 1815 to 1818 were dismayed by the contrast between Russia and the West. The year 1816 saw the establishment of the first of the secret societies that would engender the Decembrist revolt of 1825. Several of Pushkin's friends, including Pushchin and Küchelbecker, were members of these societies, but Pushkin was not. The Decembrists drew inspiration from his poems, but they did not involve him directly – probably because he was impulsive, careless and outspoken.

Pushkin was indeed anything but a born conspirator – he made his revolutionary sympathies only too obvious. On one evening in early 1820 he walked around the stalls of the Imperial Theatre carrying a portrait of a French saddler by the name of Louvel with the inscription 'A Lesson to Tsars'; earlier that year, Louvel had killed the Duc de Berry, the heir to the Bourbon throne. Not surprisingly, Pushkin's behaviour – and his writings – came to the attention of the authorities.

Alexander I and his most influential minister, the reactionary Count Arakcheyev, wanted to banish Pushkin to Siberia or to the Solovetsky monastery on the White Sea. In April 1820 Count Miloradovich, the military governor of St Petersburg, sent a police spy to Pushkin's apartment when he was out. This spy tried to bribe Pushkin's valet, Nikita Kozlov, to loan him his master's poems. Nikita told Pushkin about this on his return, and Pushkin promptly burned the manuscripts of his more dangerous poems. The following day, Miloradovich summoned Pushkin and asked to see his manuscripts. Saying he had burned them, Pushkin offered to write his poems down from memory and promptly filled an entire notebook. This was a disarmingly bold gesture, but Pushkin was also seizing the opportunity to make it clear that a number of seditious poems circulating under his name were not actually his at all; he wrote these poems down separately. Won over by Pushkin's spirit and charm, Miloradovich pardoned him then and there. The Tsar, however, refused to ratify this pardon. Only after the intervention of a number of Pushkin's most influential friends – including, eventually, the dowager Empress herself – did the Tsar relent. Rather than being sent to the remote Solovetsky monastery, Pushkin was exiled to the south of Russia and transferred from the Foreign Ministry to the 'Board of Protection of Foreign Colonists in South Russia'. There he was to serve under General Inzov.

This was the first of many occasions when Pushkin was to be saved by his friends. Unlike many children of emotionally distant parents, he had a gift for finding substitute parents who were both affectionate and reliable. This may, perhaps, point to an underlying good sense in him that can easily be overlooked. Pushkin's life – even in these years – was not only a matter of gambling, drinking, duelling, whoring and theatre going. He was in regular contact with most of the important writers of his day; in their company he evidently became more sober, more mature.

One particularly gifted friend was Pyotr Chaadaev – a Hussar colonel who was later to emerge as an important thinker about Russia's historical destiny. According to a contemporary who knew both Pushkin and Chaadaev, 'Chaadaev forced him to think. Pushkin's French education was counteracted by Chaadaev, who already knew Locke and substituted analysis for frivolity [...] He thought about things Pushkin had never thought about [...] Pushkin talked seriously with him.'

And during one of his many convalescences Pushkin read the first eight volumes of Karamzin's *History of the Russian State*, which had been published in 1818. Pushkin was critical of Karamzin's conservative views, but this did not prevent him from being fascinated by the historical material itself. 'Ancient Russia seems to have been discovered by Karamzin, as America was discovered by Columbus,' he remarked. Pushkin's interest in history was to grow ever more important over the years.

The South
1820–4

My hour of freedom, is it coming?
I call to it: it's time, it's time!
Above the sea, forever roaming,
I beckon every sail and clime.

Eugene Onegin, I, 50

Pushkin's southern exile began badly. During his first weeks in Yekaterinoslav (now Dnepropetrovsk) he seems to have tried hard to offend people, going so far as to attend one dinner in transparent muslin trousers and without underwear. The wife of the town's civil governor led her three young daughters out of the room. Not long after this occasion, Pushkin went down with fever.

Once again, he was rescued by friends. On his journey south, he had stopped in Kiev and stayed with Nikolai Raevsky, a friend from St Petersburg. Nikolai's father, General Raevsky, was a hero of the Napoleonic Wars; he and Pushkin seem to have taken to each other at once and it had been agreed that General Raevsky should ask General Inzov to allow Pushkin to accompany the family on a journey to the Caucasus and the Crimea. Towards the end of May 1820, Pushkin and the Raevskys set off.

The three months Pushkin spent with this family were unusually happy. His friendship with the kind and reliable Nikolai deepened. Alexander – Nikolai's intelligent, though cynical, elder brother – introduced Pushkin to the poetry of Byron, in French translation. And Pushkin fell in love with the elder daughter, Yekaterina; she was already informally engaged, but this does not seem to have lessened his enjoyment of her company. Pushkin himself wrote of these months, in a letter to his brother Lev:

> My friend, the happiest moments of my life have been those that I spent in the midst of the family of the honoured Raevsky. I did not see in him the hero, the glory of the Russian army; I loved him as a man with a clear mind and a simple and beautiful soul, as an indulgent, solicitous friend, as a host who is always kind and affectionate. His elder son is going to be more than merely well known. All his daughters are charming; the eldest is an unusual woman. Judge whether I was happy: a free and untroubled life in the circle of a kind family – the kind of life I love so much and that has never before been mine to enjoy; a happy, southern sky; charming surroundings; scenery which gratifies the imagination: mountains, orchards, the sea.

During the next two years Pushkin wrote two narrative poems that incorporate impressions from this journey: *The Captive of the Caucasus* and *The Fountain at Bakhchisaray*. These two poems are usually described as 'Byronic', and they are indeed imbued with some of the exoticism of Byron's 'Oriental Tales'. Even at this early stage in his career, however, Pushkin surpassed Byron. There is less rhetoric; there are more vivid, unexpected details. And, unlike Byron, Pushkin did not take himself too seriously – as we can see from some of his exchanges with his friend and fellow-poet Prince Vyazemsky. Pushkin wrote, for example, apropos these two lines from *The Captive of the Caucasus* – 'Whose passionate embrace is more alive / Than your incisive kisses?' – that he wanted it understood that 'my Georgian bites when she kisses'.

During Pushkin's absence, General Inzov's office had been transferred from Yekaterinoslav to Kishinev. Pushkin arrived there in late September 1820 and was to remain there for most of the next three years. Now the capital of Moldova, Kishinev was then the capital of Bessarabia, a region that had been ceded to Russia by Turkey only in 1812. Most of the 20,000 inhabitants were Moldavians, but there were also communities of Jews, Bulgarians, French, Italians, Greeks, Turks, Ukrainians, Germans and Albanians. The Russians were mostly military personnel and civil servants.

Pushkin saw Kishinev as dull and dirty – 'an accursed town'. Wine, women and gambling still took up much of his time, and he was – as always – short of money. His sexual affairs seem to have brought him little joy – though he had the excitement of sleeping with Calypso Polychroni, a Greek courtesan who claimed, almost certainly falsely, that her first lover had been Lord Byron. As for duelling, Pushkin seems to have shown more bravado than ever; on one occasion he arrived with a hatful of cherries, eating them while his opponent took the first shot. Pushkin was fortunate that General Inzov treated him warmly and with indulgence. He pardoned him most of his transgressions; twice, when it was impossible for him to do nothing, he placed Pushkin under house arrest, temporarily confiscating his boots.

One of Pushkin's most memorable meetings during his first year was with Colonel Pestel, the leader of the southern society of the young radical officers later to be known as the Decembrists; Pushkin described him as the most intelligent man he had ever met. Pushkin also met many other future Decembrists during a two-month stay in Kamenka, an estate belonging to a half-brother of General Raevsky; like their St Petersburg counterparts, however, the conspirators did not take him into their counsel.

During this period Pushkin was often depressed, and the poetry he wrote is a little disappointing; it has neither the sparkle of *Ruslan and Lyudmila* nor the depth of his later work. 'The Dagger' (1821) is an oddly thoughtless glorification of political murder; Pushkin seems to take it for granted that daggers will be used only against evil tyrants. His most enjoyable Kishinev poem is perhaps the *Gavriiliada* (or 'Gabriliad') – a travesty of the Annunciation in which Mary is bedded first by Satan, then by the Archangel Gabriel and lastly by God in the guise of a white dove; in its blend of the blasphemous and the erotic, it is reminiscent of Pushkin's Lycée poems – more Voltairean than Byronic. Needless to say, it was not published in Pushkin's lifetime; it did, however, occasion Pushkin great trouble when a manuscript came to the attention of the authorities in 1828.

In summer 1823 Pushkin's St Petersburg friends, Vyazemsky and Alexander Turgenev, succeeded in getting Pushkin transferred to Odessa – to the Chancery of Count Mikhail Vorontsov, who had been appointed governor-general of 'New Russia and of Bessarabia', i.e. of most of southern Russia. Vorontsov was a wealthy, English-educated liberal with a fine library, and Odessa was a cosmopolitan city, with theatres, good restaurants and a well-known opera house.

The year Pushkin spent in Odessa, however, was important, above all, for two love affairs. The poems they inspired are among the greatest love poems in any European language. Their perfect fusion of sound and meaning, however, makes them difficult to translate; they are little known to English readers.

Amalia Riznich, the wife of an Odessa shipping merchant, was a tall, graceful woman; she is described as having fiery eyes, an unusually white neck and a plait of black hair nearly five feet long. She was pregnant when Pushkin first met her, and in early 1824 she gave birth to a son. Pushkin's affair with her was brief; she had many admirers and she evoked intense jealousy in Pushkin. In May 1824 she left Odessa, and a year later she died in Italy, probably of consumption. One of Pushkin's most famous poems evokes both their parting in Odessa and her subsequent death beneath 'an eternally blue sky'. The poem ends with moving simplicity; the speaker seems unable to comprehend the finality of death:

Your sufferings, your beauty
Are now just ash and dust;
But the sweet kiss of our next tryst –
Where is it now? You owe it me.

Still more important to Pushkin was Yelizaveta Vorontsova, the wife of Pushkin's boss. Pushkin often drew portraits of women in his manuscripts – and there is no one whom he drew more often than Elise, as he called her. Their relationship, however, was brief and much interrupted. Elise gave birth to a son in late October, and it was impossible for Pushkin to see her in the last weeks of her pregnancy or the first weeks after she had given birth; during this period he made seventeen drawings of her. They may have become lovers in early February 1824, but first Pushkin and then Elise was absent for much of the next two months. After Elise returned on 20th April, she and Pushkin began to meet at a seaside villa owned by a French émigré, Baron Rainaud. In the grounds was a bathing place 'shaped like a large shell, attached to the cliffs',[3] which Pushkin evoked in this fragment:

Love's shelter is always full
Of a moist and twilit cool.
The murmur of waves against
The shore is never still.

And a walk with Elise is among the inspirations for these lines from *Eugene Onegin*:

Once by the sea, a storm impending,
I recollect my envy of

> The waves, successively descending,
> Collapsing at her feet with love.
> Oh how I wished to join their races
> And catch her feet in my embraces!
>
> *Eugene Onegin*, I, 33

His relationship with Elise brought Pushkin two enemies: Alexander Raevsky and Count Vorontsov himself. Alexander Raevsky – the elder son of General Raevsky and the man who had first introduced him to the work of Byron – had also been having an affair with Elise. Wanting to divert attention from himself, he encouraged her to spend time with Pushkin. Realising too late that Pushkin was a serious rival, he then did his best to turn Vorontsov against him. This was not difficult; Vorontsov did not object to his wife having affairs, but he saw Pushkin as a social inferior – a mere clerk with ideas above his station. He grew more and more hostile to Pushkin.

Pushkin, for his part, grew increasingly enraged by what he saw as Vorontsov's arrogance. He seems to have been all the more sensitive because he was afraid that his status as a gentleman might be compromised by his need to earn a living through writing. He had just earned 3,000 roubles for the sale of *The Fountain at Bakhchisaray* – more than any previous Russian writer had ever received for a single work. As Russia's first truly professional writer, Pushkin was in an awkward position. On the one hand, he was clear-headed about his need to earn money from writing; in 'A Conversation between a Bookseller and a Poet' he wrote, 'Inspiration is not for sale, but one can sell a manuscript.' On the other hand, uncertainty about his social standing – do true aristocrats write for money? – led him to appear over-insistent on his being one of the old, pre-Petrine nobility. At least some of Pushkin's friends – let alone his enemies – found this ridiculous. The poet and radical, Kondraty Ryleyev, after reading one of Pushkin's complaints about Vorontsov's treatment of 'a nobleman of 600 years standing', wrote to him, 'You have become an aristocrat; that made me laugh. [...] Here too I see a slight imitation of Byron. Be Pushkin, for God's sake. You're a fine enough fellow in your own right.' Pushkin, however, continued – throughout his life – to attach great importance to his standing as an aristocrat. In an article about Byron written in 1835, he said, 'It is said that Byron valued his genealogy more highly than his artistic creations. A very understandable sentiment.'

Relations between Pushkin and Vorontsov continued to deteriorate. Pushkin was furious when Vorontsov sent him off on a mission that he considered beneath him – gathering information about a plague of locusts. And Vorontsov, no doubt, found it intolerable to have a young clerk writing epigrams about him like the following:

> Part Black-Sea merchant, part milord,
> A half-baked sage and half-wit fool,
> A semi-scoundrel – but there's hope
> His scoundrelhood may soon be full.

Vorontsov had for some time been asking the Tsar to have Pushkin transferred, and Pushkin himself sent off an official letter of resignation on 2nd June. It took the authorities some time to decide what to do with him. Their difficulties were resolved when they found in their archives an intercepted letter in which Pushkin described himself as 'taking lessons in pure atheism' from an English philosopher. Atheism was as unacceptable as any other kind of radical thinking – even though the English philosopher concerned was, in fact, Vorontsov's doctor – and so Pushkin was dismissed from the Foreign Ministry. Instead, he was to be confined to Mikhailovskoye, the family estate in northern Russia, in the province of Pskov, which had once belonged to Abram Gannibal.

Pushkin's relationship with Elise remained important to him. Around the time of their parting she gave him a golden medallion with her portrait and an old seal ring with a Hebrew inscription. Pushkin would wear this ring for the rest of his life, and on his deathbed he gave it to Zhukovsky. One of his finest poems, 'The Talisman', is inspired by this gift. 'The Talisman' is an unusually thoughtful love poem, and at least a little of its power can be conveyed even through a prose summary.

The poem begins with an 'enchantress' entrusting the poet with a talisman. In the next two stanzas she lists everything that her talisman will *not* be able to do for him. It will not protect him from storm, illness or death; it will not make him rich; it will not release him from exile. In the final stanza she tells him in what way her talisman *will* protect him:

But when perfidious eyes
    Enchant your heart,
When lips, in darkness, touch your lips
    Without love to impart,
My talisman, love, will keep you
    From wrong that will harm you;
Against forgetting, hurt and betrayal,
    My talisman will arm you.

As well as inspiring this poem, Elise probably bore a child by Pushkin. A 'swarthy' daughter was born to her about nine months after their last meeting; and children born out of wedlock appear in several works Pushkin wrote around this time.

Pushkin and Elise continued to correspond while Pushkin was in Mikhailovskoye. When he received a letter from Elise, Pushkin would lock himself in his room with it for some time; in accord with her wishes, he would then burn the letter. One such occasion is evoked in the last lines of 'The Burnt Letter':

It's done! The dark pages curl.
On the light ash the cherished lines
Turn white... My chest tightens.

Dear ash, poor joy in my sad fate,
Stay with me always on my heart.

In December 1827, when the Vorontsovs were in St Petersburg, Pushkin and Elise were able to meet again; they had at least four trysts.

One of the many enigmas about Pushkin is the disjuncture between the apparent emptiness of much of his external life and the evident richness of his inner life. This adds to the interest of even the most superficial glimpses of Pushkin's ways of composing. We have several such glimpses from these years. The first is from an account by an official of General Inzov's who once had to share a room with Pushkin. He complained that 'some nights Pushkin did not sleep at all, wrote, moved about, declaimed, and read me his verses in a loud voice.' Another is from a reminiscence by Pushkin's friend, Colonel Ivan Liprandi. While on a journey with Pushkin, Liprandi came back late at night to their shared lodgings to find Pushkin 'sitting on a divan with his legs drawn up, surrounded by a large number of little scraps of paper'. And the following morning, he woke to find Pushkin 'wearing no clothes at all, sitting in the same place and in the same posture, again surrounded by his scraps of paper, but holding a pen in his hand with which he was beating time as he read; he was sometimes nodding his head and sometimes lifting it. When he saw that I was awake, he gathered together his bits of paper and began to dress.'

Still more interesting are Pushkin's own words about the process of composition. This paragraph from 'Egyptian Nights' (a brilliant but uncompleted work written in 1835) is clearly autobiographical:

One morning Charsky was in that state of grace when fancies outline themselves clearly before you and you discover vivid, unexpected words to embody your visions, when verses flow readily from your pen and resonant rhymes come forward to meet orderly thoughts. His soul was deep in sweet forgetfulness – and society, society's opinions and his own foibles no longer existed for him. He was writing poetry.

Pushkin's southern exile can be seen as framed by two poems addressed to other poets. In 'To Ovid' (December 1821) he compared himself to the other great poet who had been exiled to the region of the Black Sea. 'To the Sea' (late 1824) can be seen as a farewell to Romanticism, to Napoleon (who had died in 1821) and to Byron (who had died earlier in 1824). Both Napoleon and Byron had been idolised by Pushkin's generation, but every reference to them in Pushkin's work after 1824 is critical. In the second chapter of *Eugene Onegin*, for example, Pushkin wrote:

We all aspire to be Napoleons;
Two-legged creatures in their millions
Are no more than a tool for us…

Pushkin would continue to admire the wit and technical brilliance of Byron's *Don Juan*, but he would be sharply critical of the ideal represented by Byron's Childe Harold; elsewhere in *Onegin* he writes of Byron's success in 'clothing even hopeless egotism in the garb of melancholy romanticism'. 'To the Sea' is also a farewell to Pushkin's own youth and, of course, to the sea itself. The poem ends:

To wood and silent wilderness
I'll carry, hidden in my breast,
The shadow of your cliffs, your bays,
Your light, the murmur of your waves.

Mikhailovskoye
1824–6

A book, sound sleep, a fine excursion,
The purl of streams, the woodland shade,
A fresh, young kiss for his diversion
From dark-eyed, fair-complexioned maid,
A fiery steed with trusty bridle,
A fancy meal at which to idle,
A bottle of resplendent wine,
Seclusion, quiet – thus, in fine,
The life Onegin lived was sainted...

Eugene Onegin, iv, 38–9

In August 1824 Pushkin arrived in Mikhailovskoye – to join his parents, his sister Olga, and his brother Lev. Mirsky describes the surrounding region as 'a country of moderate-sized hills, of woods and meadows, of abundant rivers and beautiful lakes'. The above stanza from *Eugene Onegin* conveys at least some parts of Pushkin's life there.

Other aspects of his life, however, were more difficult; most painful of all was his relationship with his father. Pushkin had been placed 'under the supervision of the local authorities'. One local landowner, asked to keep Pushkin under observation, had sensibly refused, pleading poor health. In the end, Pushkin's father – who had always been on bad terms with his son, and who now saw him as a dangerous rebel – had accepted this responsibility. Pushkin, naturally, was enraged when he discovered his father opening his correspondence, and in late October they had a serious quarrel. The father accused Pushkin of having attacked him physically, and Pushkin sent off a desperate appeal to Zhukovsky and a letter to the provincial governor, saying that he had decided, 'for his and my own peace of mind, to ask His Imperial Majesty to deign to transfer me [i.e. as a prisoner] to one of his fortresses'. This letter may have been intended ironically, but there is no knowing what it might not have led to; fortunately, the messenger was unable to deliver it because of torrential rains. Zhukovsky behaved with his usual blend of good sense, honesty and generosity, telling Pushkin that he was as much at fault as his father, that he was a genius, that in poetry he had an 'inalienable means of rising above undeserved misfortune', and that 'he must preserve his moral dignity.' Zhukovsky also promised to speak to Pushkin's father when he next came to St Petersburg. Once again, Zhukovsky's intercession was successful; after their meeting, Sergei Lvovich withdrew from the responsibility of supervising his son and left Mikhailovskoye, together with Olga and Lev.

Even without his father, the prospect of spending a long northern winter in a small and remote manor house seems to have appalled Pushkin. The words 'manor house' may give the wrong impression; it was a one-storey wooden building, poorly furnished and in bad condition. Heating it was difficult, and Pushkin lived in a single room – his bedroom, study and dining room. He threw himself into plans for escaping abroad. First he tried to persuade Aleksey Vulf, the son of a neighbour, to obtain a foreign passport and take him abroad in the disguise of a servant. In the spring and summer of 1826, however, Pushkin was to think up another plan. He would persuade Zhukovsky of the danger posed to his life by a fictitious 'aneurysm'. Zhukovsky would obtain permission for him to travel to either Dorpat or Riga to see a doctor he knew, Ivan Moyer. From there Pushkin would escape to Europe or – better still – Moyer would testify that Pushkin's condition was so serious that he needed to go to Paris. The scheme collapsed; anxious on Pushkin's behalf, Zhukovsky persuaded Moyer to offer to travel to Pskov and perform the operation there. Pushkin then had to convince Moyer that he did not, after all, need the operation. Zhukovsky grew still more anxious; Pushkin grew still more frustrated.

Country life did, however, have compensations. When he was not plotting escape, Pushkin clearly found much to enjoy. He swam in lakes and rivers and went for regular walks and rides; he seems, throughout his life, to have been strong, fit and healthy, and he enjoyed physical activity. Later, while living in St Petersburg, he would sometimes get up early, walk the sixteen miles to Tsarskoye Selo, have lunch, wander about the parks and then walk back home again. It was often while walking or riding that he composed poetry.

The person he saw most of in Mikhailovskoye was Arina Rodionovna, the serf who had been Olga's wet-nurse and his own nurse. Pushkin's grandmother, Maria Gannibal, had offered her her freedom, but she had refused it. Her role at this time, during Pushkin's exile, can best be described as that of a housekeeper or steward. She was important to Pushkin, even if Soviet critics eager to establish Pushkin's credentials as a man of the people have exaggerated this importance. He was grateful for her maternal care, and the folk songs and tales he heard from her in Mikhailovskoye inspired the songs and verse fairy tales that he was to write in the 1830s. Pushkin also, more than once, joined the crowds of wandering beggars who gathered outside the nearby Svyatogorsk monastery. He listened to their songs, sometimes taking notes and sometimes joining in.

And there were visits from friends. Ivan Pushchin, one of his closest friends from the Lycée, unexpectedly arrived early one morning in January 1825. Pushchin found Pushkin's room in 'poetic confusion', with sheets of manuscripts lying about everywhere. At one moment, Pushkin wondered out loud whether Pushchin was involved in secret political activity but went on to say that Pushchin was right not to tell him about this: 'because of my many stupidities, I probably do not deserve your trust.' In reply Pushchin simply kissed and embraced Pushkin. Three months later, in April, Anton Delvig came to Mikhailovskoye and stayed for two weeks.

Throughout his two years in Mikhailovskoye, Pushkin saw a great deal of the Osipovs, a family who lived on the neighbouring estate of Trigorskoye. Aleksey Vulf, whom Pushkin had involved in the first of his escape plans, was the son of the house. He used to ride or walk to Trigorskoye most afternoons, usually accompanied by a couple of wolfhounds. The owner of the estate, Praskovya Osipova, was an attractive woman in her early forties; in a somewhat maternal manner she was evidently very fond of Pushkin. One of her daughters, Maria, has left us this account of Pushkin's visits: 'We would all be sitting at our work [...] Well then Pushkin arrived – and everything was turned upside down; laughter, jokes, conversation – a hubbub in every room [...] And how lively he was – he never sat still, he was always walking or running about.' It is uncertain whether Pushkin ever slept with Praskovya, but we know that he had sex with a startling number of her daughters and nieces. In the winter of 1825 he had an affair with her eldest daughter, Annette; Annette seems to have been devoted to Pushkin, but he treated her with an uncharacteristic callousness. Pushkin was also to have affairs, during the next few years, with a much younger daughter, Zizi, and a niece called Anna or, more often, Netty.

There was also another niece, Anna Petrovna Kern, who visited Trigorskoye several times. Mirsky describes her as 'a sensuous and light-hearted woman of twenty-five, who was greatly disgusted with her unhappy husband (a general in his sixties – their marriage had broken down), and had made up her mind she was going to enjoy life.' Pushkin tried to seduce her but failed, probably because he was too desperately infatuated. When she left a month later, he gave her not only a copy of the recently published first chapter of *Eugene Onegin*, but also a poem he had just written to her. This oddly abstract poem has become an anthology piece. It begins:

That moment comes to me again:
You passed before my eyes,
A fleeting vision of pure beauty,
A spirit from the skies.
tr. Antony Wood

People have often expressed shock at the very different tone of at least two references to Anna Petrovna in Pushkin's letters. In May 1826 he asked Aleksey Vulf, 'What is the Whore of Babylon Anna Petrovna doing?', and in a letter of February 1828 he mentions 'Mme Kern, whom with God's help I managed to fuck the other day'. The first of these remarks, however, needs to be understood in the light of Pushkin's jealousy – he had just learned that Anna Petrovna was then having an affair with Aleksey. Nor is the second remark surprising – Pushkin was not used to being rejected by women and he had, no doubt, felt humiliated by Anna Petrovna. His sleeping with her several years later may well have been an act of self-assertion rather than an expression of love or desire. What is truly surprising is Praskovya Osipova's behaviour; she was to remain a loyal friend to Pushkin – in spite of all his philandering with her daughters and nieces – for the remaining twelve years of his life.

Writing about the complexities of Pushkin's sexual affairs all too easily creates the impression that there can have been room in his life for little else. In fact, Pushkin was very studious throughout most of his life – apart from his school years. He read widely, in a number of languages, and reproached other writers for not studying enough. He always spent more on books than he could afford, and by the end of his life he had accumulated a library of 4,000 volumes, in fourteen languages; while still in Odessa he once referred to himself as a 'glazier who ruins himself buying the diamonds he needs for his work'. The letters

Pushkin wrote to his brother from Mikhailovskoye are full of orders for books, and he himself said that during these two years he 'devoured books by the cartload'. His reading included Karamzin's *History of the Russian State*, books about the peasant revolts led by Pugachov and by Stenka Razin, and French translations of Tacitus, Shakespeare, the Bible and Byron's *Don Juan*. All of these are closely linked to at least some of his own work of this period. Both Shakespeare and Tacitus lie behind *Count Nulin*; Shakespeare's history plays lie behind *Boris Godunov*; and Byron's *Don Juan* – with its light-hearted wit and its free play of thought – influenced the first chapters of *Eugene Onegin*.

Pushkin completed *The Gypsies* in Mikhailovskoye, but he had begun it while still in Odessa. Its subject matter is similar to that of his two southern, 'Byronic' narratives; its style, however, is barer, and its tone bleaker. The hero, Aleko, is a disillusioned 'Childe Harold' figure – like the hero of *The Captive of the Caucasus* – but Pushkin treats him more critically. In search of freedom, Aleko joins a gypsy camp. The young Zemfira (later to be reincarnated as the heroine of Prosper Merimée's *Carmen* – and of Bizet's opera) takes him for her lover but then betrays him. In a jealous rage, Aleko kills both Zemfira and her lover. Zemfira's father exiles him from the tribe. A central theme of the poem is the nature of freedom. Zemfira's father believes that a woman is free to love whom she chooses, as the moon is free to cast her light on one cloud, then on another. His most telling criticism of Aleko – and Pushkin's most telling criticism of the Byronic ideal – is in the lines:

> Not for freedom were you born,
> You want it for yourself alone.
> tr. Antony Wood

As well as a hundred more stanzas of *Eugene Onegin*, and the drama that was to become *Boris Godunov*, Pushkin also wrote one of his best comic poems: *Count Nulin*. Several years later, he was to describe its genesis:

> Reading Lucretia [i.e. Shakespeare's *The Rape of Lucrece*], I thought: what if Lucretia had thought of slapping Tarquin in the face? [...] Maybe it would have cooled his boldness and he would have been obliged to withdraw [...] Lucrece would not have stabbed herself. [...] The world and its history would have been different. So, for the republic, the consuls, the dictators, Cato, Caesar, we have to thank an episode of seduction, similar to one which recently occurred in my neighbourhood [...] I conceived the idea of parodying history and Shakespeare, could not resist the double temptation and in two mornings finished writing this tale.

Count Nulin works perfectly on at least two levels: as a half-joking meditation on the role of chance in great events, and as a vivid, witty evocation of life on a Russian country estate.

The shorter poems Pushkin wrote in Mikhailovskoye are diverse both in tone and in subject matter – as is clear just from a few of the titles: 'A Conversation between a Bookseller and a Poet'; 'Imitations of the Koran'; 'Message to L. Pushkin'; 'Cleopatra'; 'André Chénier'; 'A scene from Faust'; 'From Voltaire'; 'Songs about Stenka Razin'. The poet Christopher Reid has translated one of the most delicate of these – a poem which may, perhaps, be about Praskovya Osipova:

> The season's last flowers yield
> More than those first in the field.
> The thoughts they rouse, sharp, sweet,
> Have an incomparable power.
> Likewise the parting hour
> As against when we merely meet.

This period also saw two important publications. Pyotr Pletnyov, a minor poet and friend of Pushkin's, brought out the first chapter of *Eugene Onegin* in early 1825; the reviews were excellent, but Pushkin did not make as much money from it as he had hoped. Pletnyov then published Pushkin's first collection of short poems early in 1826. The edition sold out within two months, earning Pushkin 7,000 roubles, ten times his former salary from the Foreign Ministry.

In November 1825 Tsar Alexander I died unexpectedly. His elder son, the Grand Duke Constantine, had already secretly renounced the throne in favour of his younger brother Nicholas, but Alexander's death was followed by an interregnum while the two brothers confirmed their plans. On the morning of 14th December a group of radical officers attempted to take advantage of the general uncertainty. Together with about 3,000 soldiers, they assembled in the centre of St Petersburg, in Senate Square, and refused to swear allegiance to Nicholas I; the soldiers were ordered to chant the slogan 'Constantine and Constitution' even though they had no idea what it meant – it has been said that they thought that *'Konstantin'* and *'Konstitutsiya'* were a husband and wife. The preparations for the revolt were muddled; the rest of the St Petersburg garrison was expected to join the rebels but failed to do so. Nicholas spent the day gathering his forces and then attacked with artillery, quickly crushing the revolt.

Five of the Decembrist leaders, including the poet Konstantin Ryleyev, were hanged, and 120 were exiled. As well as Ryleyev and his two friends from the Lycée – Ivan Pushchin and Wilhelm Küchelbecker – Pushkin personally knew at least ten more of the convicted Decembrists. Many others, under interrogation, said that they had learned Pushkin's poems by heart and had been influenced by them. A retired lieutenant-colonel, a veteran of 1812, declared, 'Who among the young with any education at all has not read and been carried away by the works of Pushkin, which breathe freedom!'[4]

Pushkin was, of course, shaken by the fate of his friends – and his own fate was yet to be decided. He had not been party to the Decembrists' plans, but he later told both Pogodin and Vyazemsky that he had intended to travel illicitly to St Petersburg in mid-December 1825 and to go straight to Ryleyev's apartment. Had he done so, he would have been with the rebels on Senate Square. What appears to have saved Pushkin was his belief in omens: hares had twice crossed his path during the evening before his intended journey to St Petersburg; the servant who was to accompany him had fallen ill; and, as Pushkin was at last about to depart, he had met a priest. Each of these events was inauspicious. The superstitions about priests and hares were common ones, and Pushkin mentions them in *Eugene Onegin*, in relation to his favourite character, Tatiana:

If it should anywhere transpire
In her excursions from the manor
For her to meet a monk in black
Or see a swift hare cross her track,
All this so terrified Tatiana,
That she with sad presentiment
Expected some adverse event.
Eugene Onegin, v, 6

Pushkin wrote this stanza soon after receiving a message about the execution of the five Decembrist leaders.

Pushkin spent the first eight months of 1826 in uncertainty. He had reason to be anxious, but he also entertained hopes of release and public success. In the end, he seems to have been saved by a conscientious police agent. Alexander Boshnyak, who had played a crucial role in informing the authorities about the Decembrists' activities in southern Russia, was ordered to gather information about Pushkin. The items of information he elicited from people in the surrounding area include: 'that Pushkin is sometimes seen in a Russian blouse and broad-brimmed hat'; 'that he does not seem to like company or to sing any seditious songs, and still less has he tried to raise the peasants'; 'that when he had ridden somewhere, he often ordered his man to let the horse go, saying that every animal deserved its freedom'; 'that he was a person who wished to distinguish himself by eccentricity, but that he was completely incapable of any course of action based on calculation'. The local priest went so far as to say that Pushkin 'meddles in nothing and is as shy as a young girl'.

Boshnyak reported that the rumours of Pushkin inciting the local peasants to rebel were entirely unjustified. Tsar Nicholas, in due course, responded by summoning Pushkin to an interview with him in Moscow. He made it clear that Pushkin was to travel as a free man, not as someone under arrest.

Tsar Nicholas, Moscow and *Boris Godunov* 1826

> Mysterious singer – me alone
> The storm has cast onto the shore.
> I stand here underneath the cliff
> And dry my robe beneath the sun
> And sing my hymns just as before.
>
> Pushkin, from 'Arion', 1827

Pushkin's fifteen-line poem 'Arion' is based on a Greek legend about a poet and singer who threw himself into the sea after being kidnapped by pirates and was then carried to safety on the back of a dolphin. In Pushkin's version there is no explicit mention of the pirates; the first lines describe the poet singing to the crew. A sudden storm wrecks the boat, and the crew and helmsman drown. The poet alone is 'cast onto the shore'.

'Arion' is about Pushkin's relationship with the Decembrists; Pushkin wrote it in July 1827, shortly after the first anniversary of the execution of the five leaders. They perish; he alone survives. The poem has often been understood as Pushkin's coded declaration of loyalty to his youthful radical ideals. It is more likely, however, that Pushkin is asserting his right to artistic freedom, his right to serve Apollo – the sun god and the god of poetry. Apollo is not mentioned by name, but his presence makes itself strongly felt: the dolphin (present in the myth even if not mentioned in the poem itself) is sacred to Apollo; Pushkin infringes the rhyme scheme with an unexpected triple rhyme on 'oln' – a sound that evokes the last two syllables of 'Apollon', as Apollo is known in Russian; and Pushkin, shortly afterwards, was to write another short poem, 'The Poet', which begins, 'Until Apollo calls the poet' and which also includes a rhyme on this same syllable.

It is even possible that 'Arion' contains a criticism of the Decembrists: just as Pushkin is Arion, so they are the pirates who kidnapped Arion and from whom he escaped only by the skin of his teeth. The Decembrists had, after all, treated Pushkin more than cavalierly – telling the authorities how much his work had influenced them, ascribing other people's poems to him, and circulating distorted, more seditious, versions of his own poems.[5]

On 8th September 1826, after his unexpected summons from the Tsar, Pushkin arrived in Moscow and went straight to the Kremlin. The interview – which lasted for an hour, with no one else present – went remarkably well. According to Pushkin, 'The Emperor received me in the kindest possible way.' The Tsar himself later recounted that he asked Pushkin what he would have done had he been in St Petersburg on 14th December 1825 (the day of the Decembrist uprising), and that Pushkin replied, 'I would have been in the ranks of the rebels.' The Tsar went on to ask Pushkin whether his way of thought had changed: would he give his word to think and act differently if he were released from exile? After a long silence Pushkin stretched out his hand to the Tsar and promised 'to become different'. The interview ended with the Tsar pardoning Pushkin, telling him he could live wherever he chose and promising to free him from having to submit his work to the censorship; he himself would be Pushkin's censor. They left Nicholas' study together. According to one account, Nicholas said to a group of waiting courtiers, 'Gentlemen, here is a new Pushkin for you. Let us forget about the old one.' According to another account, Nicholas gestured affectionately towards Pushkin and said, 'Now he's mine!' In

Russian, this last phrase sounds warmer, and less arrogant, than in English. Pushkin might have felt honoured; he might have felt he was being adopted by a new substitute father.

At a ball that evening, Nicholas told his Deputy Minister of Education that he had talked that day 'with the cleverest man in Russia'. It seems likely that the Tsar was genuinely impressed by Pushkin and was glad of the chance to display his generosity. He may also have hoped to win popularity by releasing Pushkin from exile; he may have thought it wiser to have Pushkin as an ally than an enemy; and he may have imagined himself as a great ruler, being celebrated by a great poet. As for Pushkin, there are a number of accounts, including secret police reports, of Pushkin praising the Tsar during the next few years. And in 'Stanzas', written ten weeks after this interview, Pushkin expresses the hope that Nicholas will rule with an enlightened and forgiving spirit and that he will be as great a ruler as Peter the Great – who also began his reign with bloodshed. Both flattering and demanding, the poem ends with the lines:

Be proud of your family likeness;
Be like your ancestor in everything:
Firm and inexhaustible,
Free of vindictiveness.

The poem is subtler than is first apparent. Instead of trying to gloss over the catastrophic start to Nicholas' reign, Pushkin first openly acknowledges this and then transforms an apparently bad omen into an unexpectedly positive one, telling Nicholas that, since his harsh response to a rebellion has been similar to Peter's, he now has all the more opportunity to follow Peter's example in other respects. The Russian scholar and critic Yury Lotman has suggested that Pushkin may have voiced these thoughts to the Tsar when they first met in the Kremlin.

* * *

The importance Pushkin himself attached to the interview is clear from one of the most famous of all his poems, 'The Prophet':

> I wandered in a lonely place;
> My soul's great thirst tormented me, –
> And at a crossing of the ways
> A six-winged seraph came to me. [...]
> And to my lips he bent, tore out
> My tongue, an idle, sinful thing;
> With bloody hand, in my numb mouth
> He placed a serpent's subtle sting.
> And with his sword he clove my breast,
> And took my trembling heart entire;
> A coal alight with brilliant fire
> Into my opened breast he thrust.
> In that lone place I lay as dead,
> And God's voice called to me, and said:
> 'Prophet, arise, behold and hearken:
> Over the world, by sea and land,
> Go, and fulfil my will unshaken,
> Burn with my Word the heart of man.'
> tr. Antony Wood

This poem is dated 8th September 1826. This was the date of the interview – but almost certainly not the date that Pushkin wrote the poem. He had written an early draft in Mikhailovskoye; he did not publish the poem until 1828; and he sometimes gave his poems symbolic rather than historically accurate dates. There are several accounts of Pushkin taking with him, in his pocket, an early draft of the poem – or of a related poem – that ended:

> Arise, arise, O Russian prophet,
> Put on your chasuble of shame;
> A rope already round your neck,
> Appear before the murderous Tsar.[6]

Having no idea what to expect from Nicholas, Pushkin may have been steeling himself to defiance. Knowledge of the poem's genesis, however, makes the final version seem more enigmatic than ever. Has Pushkin – between first draft and final version – performed a complete *volte-face*? Has Nicholas become an intermediary between himself and God, finding him 'at a crossing of the ways' and endowing him with new strength? Or should the poem be understood – like 'Arion' – as an assertion of the artist's freedom, of his being obedient to no laws but heavenly ones?

In 1826, Pushkin was at the peak of his popularity. He was generally acknowledged as Russia's greatest poet, and his association with the Decembrists had only added to his glamour. And there was huge interest in his still unpublished historical drama, then titled *A Comedy about Tsar Boris and Grishka Otrepyev.* No other work of Pushkin's would ever generate such anticipation.

As a young man, in St Petersburg and Odessa, Pushkin had adored theatre, opera and ballet. He was, however, critical of the crude melodrama and stilted imitations of Racine and Corneille that were the staple fare of Russian theatres. He saw most Russian drama as monotonous. European drama – he wrote in 1830 – was born in the public square, and its aim had been to please, to entertain and to astonish. When 'poets moved to the court', drama had grown pompous, rigid and moralistic.

In 1824 Pushkin had begun reading Shakespeare, in French prose translation. Pushkin greatly admired 'our father Shakespeare' and he refers in his critical articles to no less than thirteen of his plays; it seems likely that it was in order to read Shakespeare that he began seriously studying English in 1828 (in September 1825 he had written to Vyazemsky, 'I *need* English – and one of the problems with being in exile is that I have no way to study.'). For Pushkin, Shakespeare was, above all, an antidote to French culture. His breadth of emotional and religious response was an antidote to 'the demon of laughter and irony' that

Pushkin sensed in Voltaire – and he stood for freedom from the rules of French classicism. Pushkin needed formal constraints, but he preferred them to be of his own making.

While in Mikhailovskoye, Pushkin had also been reading Nikolai Karamzin, who had just published three more volumes of his *History of the Russian State*, covering the period from the death of Ivan the Terrible in 1584 to the seizure of the Russian throne by the False Dmitry in 1605. Pushkin's *Comedy*, now usually known as *Boris Godunov*, is often described as a Shakespearean treatment of the historical material in Karamzin. As always, however, Pushkin does things his own way. He follows Shakespeare in his use of blank verse and in ignoring the neo-classical unities of time, place and action, but his characteristic restraint and concision is anything but Shakespearean. Nor does Pushkin follow Karamzin blindly; his interpretation of some historical events is, in fact, opposite to Karamzin's.

Pushkin's battles to get his *Comedy* through the censorship were to play a critical role in his relationship with Tsar Nicholas. Pushkin completed it only a few days before the Decembrist uprising, and neither he nor the Tsar saw its subject matter as merely historical. The play's political resonances are complex; the plot, however, is simple: before the play begins, the Russian crown has passed to Fyodor, the mentally incapable son of Ivan the Terrible. A powerful noble, Boris Godunov, has been appointed regent. Hoping, in due course, to become Tsar, Boris has murdered Fyodor's younger brother, Dmitry.

The first act begins with Boris accepting the Russian crown with feigned reluctance. Several years later, Grigory, an ambitious young monk, realises that the murdered Dmitry would have been the same age as himself. Knowing that the Poles are eager for war with Russia, he decides to make out that the young tsarevich Dmitry, in fact, escaped from Boris' attempt to murder him – and that he himself *is* Dmitry. Grigory absconds from the monastery, crosses the frontier and is welcomed by the Polish nobility. At the head of a Polish army, Grigory – as Dmitry –

invades Russia. Boris' hold on the throne is already weak. The country has been ravaged by famine and plague, and the nobles have been plotting against him. And he is troubled by guilt; after seeing a vision of the murdered Dmitry, Boris dies.

The false Dmitry has Fyodor and his mother poisoned and seizes the throne. One of his supporters tells the crowd that Fyodor and his mother have taken their own lives; he then asks the crowd to show their support for Dmitry with a cheer of loyalty. The crowd stays silent.

This final stage direction – 'The people stay silent' – has become the most famous line in the play and is often quoted when Russians silently acquiesce in their leaders' actions, but the words are not present in any surviving manuscript. The original version ended with the people enthusiastically cheering Dmitry. This encapsulates one of the elements of the play most unacceptable to the Tsarist – and, later, Soviet – censorship: Dmitry had gained the throne with Polish support, so it was unacceptable to portray him as genuinely popular with the Russian people. Some official, or even Nicholas himself, may have suggested 'The people stay silent' as a compromise; Pushkin may have thought it up himself, remembering a similar moment in Shakespeare's *Richard III*; he may even have written it tongue-in-cheek, hoping people would understand that it was he himself who had been forced into silence. There may be truth in all these suggestions.

This final stage direction was far from being the only controversial element in Pushkin's *Comedy*. Even at this stage in his career, Pushkin was a scrupulous historian – and he saw no necessary conflict between the demands of theatre and the demands of scholarship. As well as reading Karamzin, he had consulted medieval chronicles and uncensored foreign accounts of the Time of Troubles which make it clear that the Russian people were hostile towards Boris Godunov and welcoming towards Dmitry. Pushkin had also read papers belonging to his own family. Several Pushkins had played public roles during this period, and Pushkin included two of them in his play. One of them, Afanasy Pushkin, even makes an eloquent speech attacking autocracy and serfdom. Pushkin had come to the correct but – at the time – controversial conclusion that Dmitry's popularity resulted, at least in part, from his promise to abolish serfdom, which Boris had recently tightened; no historian before Pushkin had written about this.

During September and October 1826, Pushkin gave at least five readings from *A Comedy about Tsar Boris and Grishka Otrepyev* in the apartments of Moscow friends. These readings made a deep impression on Pushkin's audiences; they understood the play as inventive and original, revolutionary in its form and radical in its politics. Mikhail Pogodin, later a well-known historian, recorded the reaction of an audience that included Pyotr Chaadaev and several other important writers and thinkers. The reading began late one morning:

Instead of the high-flown language of the gods, we heard simple, clear, ordinary, but at the same time – poetic, captivating speech! [...] When Pushkin came to Pimen's account of Ivan the Terrible's visit to the Kirillov monastery, and of how the monks 'prayed Almighty God / to take compassion on his storm-tossed soul', we simply somehow lost consciousness. One person felt feverish; another felt chilled. People's hair stood on end. [...] One moment someone would suddenly leap to his feet, another moment someone would suddenly cry out. Now silence, now an explosion of exclamations [...] The reading ended. We looked at each other for a long time and then threw ourselves at Pushkin. There were embraces, a hubbub, laughter, flowing tears, congratulations. Champagne appeared, and Pushkin became animated, seeing what an effect he had had on the young people gathered there. [...] Then Pushkin began telling us about the scene between Marina Mniszech and the Pretender, which he had composed on horseback and half of which he had then forgotten, which he deeply regretted. O, what an astonishing morning that was, leaving traces that remained for the rest of one's life. I don't know how we separated, how we got through the rest of the day, how we went to bed. It's unlikely any of us slept that night. Our entire organism was so shaken.

At least for some months after his return from exile, Pushkin was idolised. His mere appearance in the stalls of a Moscow theatre was enough to evoke a general buzz of excitement. And, as we have seen, his meeting with the Tsar seemed to promise a profound change in his relationship with the authorities. Gradually, however, Pushkin must have realised that his life had not changed as much as he had hoped. His first disappointments relate to the censorship of his *Comedy*.

The Tsar's promise to be his personal censor was not what it had first seemed. Pushkin was to submit his work to the Tsar not directly, but through an intermediary – Count Benckendorff, who was head of both the *gendarmerie* (a uniformed and well-armed police force) and of the 'Third Department' (Nicholas' newly established secret police). Benckendorff's attitude towards Pushkin was one of hostile contempt – and in reality it was he, rather than Nicholas, who was to be Pushkin's censor.

Hearing that Pushkin had been reading the play to friends, Benckendorff expressed astonishment that he had not first submitted the text to the Tsar. Pushkin promptly sent Benckendorff the manuscript and asked him to do this on his behalf. The Tsar's response was as follows: 'I consider that Mr Pushkin's aim would be attained if, after purging it as necessary, he made his *Comedy* into an historical tale or romance after the manner of Walter Scott.' The Tsar's suggestion is not unperceptive – Pushkin did, after all, write a historical novel less than ten years after this – but it was deeply upsetting to Pushkin, whose ambition was no less than to reform Russian drama. It would be six years before a castrated version of Pushkin's *Comedy* was published, and it was first approved for performance only in 1870. Mussorgsky's great opera, with a libretto deriving largely from Pushkin's play and partly from Karamzin, was first performed in 1874.

Pushkin was, of course, still an object of suspicion for many other reasons. The death penalty had been abolished in Russia in 1753 (except for murder or attempted murder of members of the imperial family), and Nicholas' execution of the Decembrist leaders had shocked many people. The repercussions of the uprising were to continue for many years. Pushkin regularly attended the salon of Princess Zinaida Volkonskaya, whose Decembrist brother, Sergei Volkonsky, was by then in exile. In late December, Pushkin attended an emotional party in honour of Sergei's wife, Maria (née Raevskaya); it was with Maria and her family that Pushkin had travelled around Crimea and the Caucasus at the beginning of his southern exile. Maria was now on her way – against the wishes of both her father and the Tsar – to join her husband in Siberia. Pushkin intended to give her a poem to take with her, but he was unable to finish it in time. A week later, he entrusted two poems to Alexandra Muravyova, another Decembrist wife about to set out on the same long and difficult journey. The better known of the two poems, 'Deep in Siberian mines', is addressed to the exiled Decembrists as a group. A bold gesture of solidarity, it ends:

Your heavy fetters will fall off;
Your prisons crumble – bolt and ward.
Freedom will greet you by the door
And brothers give you back your sword.

The other, less-known poem is addressed to Ivan Pushchin. It begins with Pushkin's recollection of Pushchin being the first of his friends to visit him when he was himself in exile in Mikhailovskoye, in January 1825:

First friend, friend beyond price,
One morning I blessed fate
When sleigh bells, your sleigh bells
Sang out and filled my lonely home
Lost in its drifts of snow.

May my voice now, please God,
Gladden your soul
In that same way
And lighten your exile
With light from our Lycée's clear day.

Pushkin grew more conservative over the years, and his attitude to the Decembrists has been much argued about. On the one hand, he claimed in one of his last poems, *'Exegi monumentum'*, that he is dear to the people because 'in my harsh age I sang of liberty.' On the other hand, he quickly came to see the rebellion as futile and to feel appalled at how close he had been to sharing the Decembrists' fate. The manuscript of chapter five of *Eugene Onegin* includes sketches of gallows with five dangling corpses and the words: 'And I too, like a fool, could have…'

In late 1826, however, Pushkin seems, for the main part, to have behaved cautiously – and to have felt genuinely grateful towards the Tsar. The poem addressed to Pushchin is evidence not so much of political commitment as of loyalty to a friend. 'Deep in Siberian mines' is more obviously political, but it is Pushkin's only poem or recorded statement in this vein. He was lucky, though, that it was never seen by Benckendorff's agents.

Bachelor Life
1826−9

City of splendour, city of poor,
Spirit of grace and servitude,
Heaven's vault of palest lime,
Boredom, granite, bitter cold –
Still I miss you rather, for
Down your streets from time to time
One may spy a tiny foot,
One may glimpse a lock of gold.
Pushkin, 'City of Splendour', 1828, tr. Antony Wood

The euphoria evoked in Pushkin by the Tsar's pardon soon gave way to frustration. During the next few years Pushkin moved restlessly between Moscow and St Petersburg. His difficulties with the authorities continued. As well as being unable to publish his *Comedy*, he twice got into trouble because of poems he had written many years before. Lines excised by the censor from his 1825 elegy about the executed French poet, André Chénier, had circulated in manuscript; in 1827 they came to the attention of the authorities and were understood to be about the Decembrist revolt – even though they had been written before it. Pushkin cleared up the confusion but was reprimanded all the same. Still more serious difficulties arose in 1828 over another poem: the *Gavriiliada*, Pushkin's 1821 blasphemous version of the Annunciation story. When a copy of this came to the attention of Benckendorff and the Tsar, Pushkin denied authorship. It was all too obvious, however, that he was lying, and in the end he had to admit this to the Tsar.

Pushkin wanted more stability in his life but was unable to achieve it. The deepest of his frustrations was probably his inability – for all his fame – to find a wife. While continuing to enjoy affairs as in the past, he courted several women with a view to marriage. In late 1826 he courted Sofya Pushkina, a distant relative already all but engaged to another man; his failure with her was perhaps not surprising. He also seems to have found it easy to get over his second failure – with Sofya Urusova, who may have become the Tsar's mistress. A third woman, Yekaterina Ushakova, seems to have returned his feelings, but this time it was Pushkin who lost interest. He did, however, remain friends with both Yekaterina and her younger sister, Yelizaveta, and he was to carry on seeing them during visits to Moscow over the next few years. The two sisters teased him over his inconstancy, and he evidently did not try to defend himself. He made as many as eighty drawings in Yelizaveta's album – and in 1829 he wrote in it what has become known as his 'Don Juan list': the names of twenty-one women with whom he had been somewhat involved, and then – separately – the names of his sixteen most important women. This second part of the list ended with the name of his future wife.

In St Petersburg, he fell in love with, and proposed to, Annette Olenina: a graceful, nineteen-year-old blonde. She was flattered by Pushkin's interest, but she did not see him as a desirable husband. She wrote in her diary of his 'dreadful side-whiskers, dishevelled hair, nails like claws, small stature, affected manners, and arrogant attitude towards the women he chose to love…' It is unlikely that her parents were any more enthusiastic; the Olenins were an important family – and Pushkin was known to be a gambler, a rake, politically suspect, and with little in the way of a reliable income.

It was around this time that Pushkin wrote his finest – and perhaps most untranslatable – love lyric; it may have been occasioned by Annette's rejection of him. This eight-line poem begins with absolute simplicity – 'I loved you' – and moves delicately towards a greater complexity of thought and syntax. The literal meaning of the final two lines is: 'I loved you so sincerely, so tenderly as God grant you be loved by another.' Two contradictory meanings are held in perfect balance. A generous wish – *may you find true love!* – coexists with a harsh warning or even threat – *you will never find anyone who will love you as truly as I did.* The American translator Michele A. Berdy has written:

Pushkin makes the greatest sacrifice a lover can make – wishing that his beloved will be loved again. At the same time, he implies that this will never happen. The poem is a cry of hurt; he is wishing her well and wishing her ill all at the same time.

At the end of December 1828, at a Moscow ball, Pushkin met the young woman he would eventually marry: Natalya Goncharova. She was sixteen, tall, auburn-haired and unusually beautiful; she clearly made an immediate impression on Pushkin. Soon after this, Pushkin left Moscow for St Petersburg, but he returned to Moscow in early March. On 1st May 1829 he asked, through an intermediary, for Natalya's hand. Her mother told him that her daughter was still young, and that it was too early to take such a decision. Pushkin thanked her 'for allowing him hope' – and immediately left Moscow to spend four months in Transcaucasia. In the autumn he returned to Moscow for three weeks. He paid visits to Natalya and her family, but he seems to have felt ill at ease with them and to have spent more time with the Ushakov sisters. In St Petersburg that winter he had an affair with Karolina Sobańska, a tall, striking Polish woman he had first met in Odessa. Sophisticated, intelligent and sexually experienced, she was everything that Natalya was not. There is no reason to think that Pushkin wanted to marry her, but she vividly represented everything about his bachelor life that he was most reluctant to relinquish. For around two months he appears not to have known what to do. Back in Moscow in March 1830, he seems, at least briefly, to have done his best to sabotage his courtship, telling both Natalya and her mother about his obsession with Sobańska.

One way Pushkin tried to escape his troubles during these years was through gambling. He was now losing large sums – 6,000 roubles to one young man at the St Petersburg English club in the spring of 1829, and nearly 25,000 roubles to a professional gambler in Moscow not long afterwards. This was far more than he was ever likely to earn from his writing – even his successful 1826 collection of short poems had brought him only 7,000 roubles – and he was amassing huge debts. His behaviour – which amounted to what would now be called an addiction – alarmed his friends. In March 1829, after Pushkin had left St Petersburg for Moscow, Sofya Karamzina (the daughter of the historian, herself a perceptive, if acerbic, letter-writer) wrote, 'We were not sorry to see him go, since he had become unpleasantly morose in society, gambling day and night with, it is said, a gloomy rage.' Pushkin himself evokes the self-punishing world of the serious gambler in the epigraph of his novella *The Queen of Spades*:

In rainy weather
They gathered together
    To play.
To double – redouble –
A stake was no trouble,
    They say.
They did not find it hard
To entrust to a card
    Their pay,
So no day of rain

Ever slipped by in vain,
   They say.

In his attempts to escape his troubles, Pushkin also asked several times to be allowed to travel. In 1828, after Russia declared war on Turkey, Pushkin applied to join the army. When Benckendorff refused, he asked for permission to travel to Paris. This time Benckendorff persuaded Pushkin to withdraw his request. Protocol did not allow Benckendorff to refuse Pushkin without consulting the Tsar – and the Tsar was at the Front.

Pushkin's spring 1829 journey to the Caucasus was without official permission; the war with Turkey was not yet over, and Pushkin wanted at least to witness it. In mid-June he caught up with the Russian army as it advanced west into what is now Chechnya. His old friend Nikolai Raevsky promptly presented him to the commander-in-chief, Field Marshal Paskevich. Paskevich welcomed Pushkin, unaware that he was there without permission and hoping that he would write about the campaign. The following day, in response to a Turkish attack, Pushkin ran out of the headquarters, mounted a horse and was quickly among the outposts. An official report describes 'how an experienced officer, sent after the poet [...] overtook him, with difficulty, and removed him by force from the Cossack front line just as Pushkin, animated by the courage one sees in a new recruit, seized a lance from one of the dead Cossacks and galloped against the enemy cavalry'. Pushkin was, apparently, mistaken for a mad German priest; his excitement at the time was almost certainly genuine, but there is irony in the small pen-and-ink self-portrait he drew later that year in Yelizaveta Ushakova's album: a man, on horseback, carrying a lance and wearing a round hat and a cloak. Later in June, along with the Russian army, Pushkin entered the town of Erzerum; this was to be his only experience of life outside Russia. Seven years later, Pushkin was to publish *Journey to Erzerum* – an unconventional, semi-fictionalised memoir that is still undervalued. Pushkin subtly shows how his own stereotyped understanding of 'Orientals' leads him into making a fool of himself during encounters with Turks, Persians and Kalmyks. When confronted with the reality of other ways of life, Pushkin seems to have been quick to modify his characteristic chauvinism – the chauvinism that more than once upset Vyazemsky and his other liberal friends.

In January 1830, Pushkin asked for permission to go to France or Italy, or else to be allowed to join a Foreign Ministry mission to eastern Siberia and China. Around this time he wrote these lines:

Let's go, I'm ready. Fleeing the haughty maiden,
I'm ready, friend, to follow wherever you choose:
To the foot of the wall of distant China,
To seething Paris, or to the city where
The night-time oarsman no more sings Tasso's songs;
To fragrant cypress groves, to where the relics
Of ancient cities doze beneath their ash…
Anywhere, I'm ready… Only, tell me, my friend:
Will passion die, will I forget through travel
The proud, tormenting maiden? Or will I bring
Back love, my usual tribute, to lay before
Her feet, before her youthful anger?

After yet another refusal from Benckendorff, Pushkin seems to have understood once and for all that he would never be allowed to leave Russia.

It is hard to read about Pushkin's life during these years – his 'gloomy rage' while gambling, his inability to publish his *Comedy* – without feeling a painful sense of waste. Pushkin did, however, write a great deal during these years – including several chapters of *Onegin*, the verse narrative *Poltava*, the unfinished *The Blackamoor of Peter the Great* and several of his best lyrics. If we knew only the work, our impression would be simply of a great poet at the height of his powers, writing with clarity and unusual honesty – as in these last lines of 'Memory' (1828), a short poem about the dark thoughts that haunt the poet while the rest of the world is asleep:

In silence memory unrolls her scroll
Before me. With disgust, I read my life,
Tremble and curse, shed bitter, bitter tears,
But do not wash away the melancholy lines.

Courtship and Marriage
1830

> Blest who in youth was truly youthful,
> Blest who matured in proper time,
> Who, step by step, remaining truthful,
> Could weather, yearly, life's bleak clime,
> To curious dreams was not addicted,
> Nor by the social mob constricted,
> At twenty was a blade or swell
> And then at thirty married well...
>
> *Eugene Onegin*, VIII, 10

On 5th April 1830 Pushkin wrote to Natalya Goncharova's mother, asking once again for Natalya's hand. As a proposal of marriage, his letter is unusual; most of it is about his own inadequacies as a potential husband. Pushkin sees himself as generally unworthy of Natalya. His financial position, though adequate, will not be enough to bring Natalya a position in the world 'as brilliant as she merits'. And he hints at other anxieties that he 'cannot resolve to commit to paper'; he is probably thinking of his ambiguous position with regard to the authorities.

Pushkin may have been anxious not to deceive the Goncharovs with false promises. It is also possible, as Binyon suggests, that he may have half-hoped his proposal would be refused. Then he would be free to return to bachelor life – and Karolina Sobańska – with a clear conscience. The Goncharovs, however, were not a prominent family like the Olenins. They were short of money, and Natalya's father was mentally unstable. Probably glad of the chance to marry off one of her three daughters, Natalya's mother accepted Pushkin's proposal.

In St Petersburg high society Natalya was to win great admiration for her beauty and – according to some accounts – charm. She has had to pay for this by attracting almost universal posthumous condemnation. Mirsky's critical view of Natalya is one that has always been widely held:

She was strikingly beautiful and keenly conscious of it. She was firmly convinced of her right to a prominent place in Society on the strength of her looks, which were her only title to eminence. [...] She was quite uncultured and had no interest in the things of the mind. She was brought up in the conviction that a gentlewoman's only duty was first to catch a husband, and then to enjoy to the utmost the pleasures of Society. Even this worldly and frivolous education was only of a second-best kind. Her manners were not free from vulgarity, her coquetry was not in the best of tastes, her conversation was neither refined nor entertaining.

It is hard to judge to what extent Mirsky's scorn is justified, and to what extent it derives from intellectual snobbery. All we can be sure of is that Natalya enjoyed flirting and had no particular interest in poetry, and that this has always enraged Pushkin's admirers.

As for Pushkin himself, he clearly wanted Natalya very much – and he took his responsibilities as a husband seriously. During the next year he did all he could to put his financial and other affairs in order.

First, he wrote to his father, asking for his blessing on the marriage – and for financial help. His father, Sergei Lvovich, replied emotionally and with some generosity, at once agreeing to settle on Pushkin part of the family estate at Boldino, in the province of Nizhny Novgorod. Pushkin then wrote to Benckendorff, asking for some confirmation that he was not 'in the Emperor's disfavour'; it is possible that he was hoping to be reinstated in the Civil Service with a higher rank. Benckendorff replied politely but offered no real help.

Pushkin had already tried to regularise the income from his writing by instructing his friend and publisher Pletnyov to enter into an agreement with the St Petersburg bookseller, Smirdin. In exchange for nearly 10,000 unsold copies of the various books that Pletnyov had already published, Smirdin agreed to guarantee Pushkin 600 roubles a month for four years; this amounted to about half the value of the books.

After spending part of the summer in St Petersburg, Pushkin passed through Moscow again in late August, on his way to Boldino. The day after a ball at the Goncharovs he quarrelled with Natalya's mother; she seems to have been dictatorial and interfering, and his relations with her were to remain difficult. Uncertain whether or not his engagement had been broken off, he continued on his way.

He arrived in Boldino on 3rd September. Shortly after his arrival, strict quarantine precautions were introduced because of an outbreak of cholera. Pushkin was, in effect, confined in Boldino until the end of November. There were no social or other distractions. His only task was to have himself registered as the owner of the 200 serfs his father had given him in the neighbouring village of Kistenevo. Other than that, there was nothing to do but write – and, during the next three months, he was to write an extraordinary amount. After devoting much of December and January to continued attempts to sort out his financial situation, Pushkin married Natalya Goncharova on 18th February 1831.

A week before his marriage Pushkin wrote to an old friend, Nikolai Krivtsov:

I have calmly weighed the advantages and disadvantages of the state I am choosing. My youth has passed by noisily and fruitlessly. Until now I have lived differently from how people usually live. There has been no happiness for me. *Il n'est de bonheur que dans les voies communes.*[7] I am past thirty. At thirty, people usually get married – I am acting as people usually act, and I shall probably not regret it. Besides, I am marrying without rapture, without childish enchantment. I see the future not as full of roses, but in its austere nakedness. Sorrows will not astonish me: they are included in my family budget. Any joy will be something I did not expect.

Pushkin was uncharacteristically sad and silent during a stag party on the eve of his wedding. His sense that his youth was now over must have been strengthened by his grief for Anton Delvig, who had died of typhus only a month before. And there are two accounts of bad omens during the ceremony itself. According to one witness, not only did Pushkin knock over a crucifix but also, during the exchange of rings, one of them fell to the floor. According to another witness, a cross and a Bible fell down from the lectern while the couple were walking round it – and the candle Pushkin was carrying was blown out. Both witnesses recollect Pushkin saying the words, 'Tous les mauvais augures.'[8]

Boldino
Autumn 1830

But I was born for peaceful pleasures,
For country quiet: there I thrive:
There sounds the lyre with clearer measures.
Creative dreams are more alive.

Eugene Onegin, I, 55

A few months before his marriage, while he was trapped in Boldino by the cholera epidemic, Pushkin wrote to Pletnyov: 'Ah, my dear fellow! How charming this countryside is! Just imagine: steppe after steppe; of neighbours not a soul; ride to your heart's content; write whatever comes into your head – no one will interfere. Why, I'll cook you up a lot of all kinds of things, both prose and verse.' And in early December, shortly after his return to Moscow, Pushkin wrote to Pletnyov again:

I shall tell you (as a secret) that in Boldino I wrote as I have not written for a long time. Here is what I have brought with me: the two *last* chapters of *Onegin,* the eighth and ninth, completely ready for the press. A tale, written in *ottava rima* (of about 400 lines), which let's bring out *Anonyme.* Several dramatic scenes or little tragedies, to wit: *The Miserly Knight, Mozart and Salieri, Feast during a Plague,* and *Don Juan.* In addition to that I have written about 30 small poems. Good? That is still not all. (Completely secret – for you alone) I have written five prose tales which are making Baratynsky [another poet, a friend and rival of Pushkin's] neigh and kick about – and which we shall also publish *Anonyme.*

One way or another, Pushkin was imprisoned throughout his adult life, and most of the time he was struggling to escape. It had been no different in Boldino; Pushkin had kept trying to return to Moscow but had been repeatedly turned back at quarantine roadblocks. Often, however – and not only in Boldino – Pushkin was at his most creative when most confined. The liberation he sometimes found in confinement is encapsulated in a striking story about him as a young man in St Petersburg:

Nikita Vsevolozhsky [the founder of *The Green Lamp*] had an old valet, someone very devoted but extremely obstinate. He heard Pushkin complaining about a publisher who was demanding the conclusion of a poem for which he had already paid Pushkin. Once Pushkin called round when Nikita was out. The old valet seized the opportunity and kept telling Pushkin he must finish the poem. Pushkin got angry and told him he was never going to finish it. The obstinate old man [...] locked Pushkin into Nikita's study. Whatever Pushkin said or did [...], the old valet just went on repeating: 'Write your verses, Alexander Sergeich. I'm not going to let you out as you wish. You have to write – so write!' Realising that the valet was not going to let him out until Nikita returned in the evening, Pushkin sat down at the desk and got so carried away that he went on writing until the next day, telling both the valet and Nikita himself to leave him in peace. And so Pushkin finished one of his long poems.[9]

Pushkin's creativity during this 'confinement' in Boldino is astonishing. His works of this period – which also include the first of his verse fairy tales, 'The Tale of the Village Priest and his Workman Balda' – are varied in tone, structure and subject matter. The slightest of the works listed above is the tale in *ottava rima*, 'The Little House in Kolomna' – a comic story about a widow who hired a cook who asked no money for her work. In the end the cook turns out to be a Hussar. So apparently inconsequential that it could almost be called absurdist, this was the inspiration for Stravinsky's comic opera *Mavra*.

The *Little Tragedies* – none more than a few hundred lines long – are highly focused studies of psychological states. The 'dramatic scenes' of Bryan Procter, a now almost forgotten English writer who published under the pseudonym of Barry Cornwall, were an important inspiration. *A Feast in Time of Plague*, however, is freely adapted from a play by another forgotten English writer, John Wilson. The most famous passage in Pushkin's play is the following:

There is joy in battle,
Poised on a chasm's edge,
And in black ocean's rage –
That whirl of darkening wind and wave –
In an Arabian sandstorm,
And in a breath of plague.

Within each breath of death
Lives joy, lives secret joy
For mortal hearts, a pledge,
Perhaps, of immortality,
And blessed is he who, storm-tossed,
Can see and seize this joy.

This song – not a translation but an original composition of Pushkin's – is a powerful evocation of the ecstatic joy that a compulsive gambler can take in self-destruction, and it exemplifies the clarity with which Pushkin writes even about the darker aspects of human nature. The plight of the revellers – threatened by a dangerous epidemic – does also, of course, reflect Pushkin's own situation in Boldino.

The Miserly Knight is about a father who is reluctant to help his son out financially, even though he could afford to do so; Pushkin's own father – at least in Pushkin's view – had behaved similarly. It was probably to prevent gossip about their relationship that Pushkin pretended, when first publishing this play in 1836, to have translated it from English.

The most famous of the *Little Tragedies* is *Mozart and Salieri* (which gave Peter Shaffer the idea for *Amadeus*). Envious of Mozart's apparently effortless success, Pushkin's Salieri questions whether justice exists in the universe; in the end he murders Mozart – as, in Pushkin's day, he was widely believed to have done.

Pushkin has often been compared to Mozart. His Mozartian facility – the sustained intensity of inspiration that allowed him to compose masterpiece after masterpiece in quick succession – was never more evident than during his two 'Boldino Autumns', in 1830 and 1833. Pushkin, however, was not only the Mozart we see in his play; he was also the diligent, hard-working Salieri. One of his greatest works, *The Bronze Horseman*, was the fruit not only of sudden inspiration during the second 'Boldino Autumn' but also of a decade's study of Peter the Great; *The Captain's Daughter*, the most subtle and poetic of all nineteenth-century Russian novels, also has its origins in painstaking historical research.

The Stone Guest, the longest of the *Little Tragedies*, is based on the Don Juan story. Here the autobiographical element is still more obvious; in a letter of April 1830, Pushkin had written that Natalya is 'my one hundred and thirteenth love'. Once again, though, features of Pushkin can be seen in both of the protagonists. Just as Pushkin is not only Mozart but also Salieri, so he is not only Don Juan but also Don Alvaro (Pushkin's Don Alvaro or 'stone guest' is not the father but the husband of

Dona Ana). Pushkin is, after all, about to become the husband of a much younger and very beautiful wife – as Don Alvaro was before his death at the hands of Don Juan.

This confrontation between Death and Love relates to Pushkin's experience of these months in more ways than is obvious. Firstly, Vasily Lvovich, Pushkin's uncle, died in late August; had it not been for the ensuing period of mourning, Pushkin might have been able to marry in September. Secondly, the cholera epidemic was extremely dangerous; the following year it would kill 7,000 people in St Petersburg alone. While Pushkin was in Boldino, he learned that the disease had reached Moscow. The post was delayed by the quarantine road blocks; as a result, Pushkin received no letters from Natalya for several weeks and grew very anxious about her safety.

At the same time as worrying about Natalya, Pushkin was saying goodbye to ghosts from his past. It was in Boldino that he wrote his last poem to Amalia Riznich, reproaching her for being unable – because of her death – to give him the kiss that she owed him. He also wrote a bleak farewell to Elise Vorontsova. After admitting to her that each of their images has faded, or grown dark – 'clothed in the darkness of the tomb' – in the heart of the other, he asks her to accept 'his heart's greeting':

Like a friend who wordlessly embraces
A friend about to be confined.

These last two lines constitute a precise, though veiled reminiscence. In October 1827, Pushkin had stopped at a post station on the way from Petersburg to Mikhailovskoye; he had found a copy of Schiller's *The Visionary* there and had been reading it when some prisoners arrived under escort. Among these prisoners Pushkin had, with difficulty, recognised his Lycée friend, the Decembrist Wilhelm Küchelbecker, who had spent most of the preceding two years in solitary confinement; Küchelbecker had himself been something of a visionary.

Pushkin and Küchelbecker had embraced – and been dragged apart by policemen.

Küchelbecker – who by 1830 had been transferred to Siberia – is another of the ghosts to whom Pushkin is saying goodbye during his enforced stay in Boldino. Küchelbecker's sudden appearance in the last lines of the love poem is startling; it is as if Pushkin wants us to feel his own shock at Küchelbecker's sudden appearance in the post station. It is still more startling to realise that the implication of these two lines is that it is Pushkin himself who is about to be confined. The poem, we realise, can be read as the last words of a Don Juan whose hand has already been taken by the Stone Guest, a Don Juan already slipping into the underworld. The implication may even be that Dona Ana and the Stone Guest are the same person; that to be married is to be removed from the world like Küchelbecker, to be confined in a stone prison.

The *Little Tragedies* are – for the main part – written in the barest of styles, free of the rhetoric that has often passed for poetry. It is perhaps not surprising that Pushkin should have written his first complete work of prose fiction, *The Tales of Belkin* – as well as the related, but unfinished, 'History of the Village of Goryukhino' – at more or less the same time. He had already made several false starts at writing prose, including *The Blackamoor of Peter the Great*. As early as 1822, however, he had had a clear idea of what he wanted: 'Precision and brevity are the most important qualities of prose. Prose demands thoughts and more thoughts – without thoughts, dazzling expressions serve no purpose.'

The five tales were purportedly told by a number of different people to a fictitious small landowner, Ivan Petrovich Belkin; Belkin has written them down and, after his death, the manuscript has fallen into the hands of a fictitious editor, 'A.P.' The stories are concise, and there is little by way of psychological explanation. Their apparent simplicity, however, imbues them with great suggestive power. Important questions are raised about such matters as fate, justice, honour and fidelity. At the same time, Pushkin plays with the reader's expectations, parodying a variety of writers and genres – from the Gothic tale and the sentimental story to the historians Nikolai Karamzin and Nikolai Polevoy.

Pushkin seems to have hoped that *The Tales of Belkin* would be a popular success and that he might earn as much as 10,000 roubles (in the event he earned less than 5,000). At the same time, he was clearly aware that these tales were too sophisticated for his audience. In a brief article published only a few months earlier, he wrote:

England is the fatherland of caricature and parody [...] Walter Scott was once shown some verses purported to have been composed by him. 'They seem to be my verses,' he said with a laugh. 'I write so much, and I've been writing so long, that I can't deny even this piece of nonsense.' I don't think that any one of our well-known writers would see himself in the parodies printed in any of the Moscow journals. This kind of joke requires a rare flexibility of style; a good parodist is a master of all styles, but our parodists can hardly master even just one.

Nearly 150 years after Pushkin's first 'Boldino Autumn' Andrey Sinyavsky wrote:

Pushkin is the golden mean of Russian literature. Having kicked Russian literature headlong into the future, he himself swung backwards and now plays in it more the role of an eternally flowering past to which it returns in order to become younger. The moment a new talent appears, there we see Pushkin with his prompts and crib notes – and generations to come, decades from now, will again find Pushkin standing behind them. If we take ourselves back in thought to far-off times, to the sources of our native tongue, there too we will find Pushkin – further back still, earlier still, on the eve of the first chronicles and songs. An archaic smile plays on his lips.[10]

For a more complete understanding of what Sinyavsky means by this, we need only look at the role played in literary history by a single short poem written in Boldino: 'The Demons'. In 1918 the poet Alexander Blok published *The Twelve*, a part comic, part ecstatic, part sinister evocation of revolutionary Petrograd; twelve Red Guards are striding through a blizzard at the heels of Jesus Christ. In 1872 Dostoevsky published *The Demons*, a fiercely critical examination of the conspiratorial whirl of the Russian revolutionary circles in which he had once himself been involved; his title was intended to evoke Pushkin's poem. And in 1836 Pushkin himself published *The Captain's Daughter*, a historical novel set against the background of a peasant rebellion that is seen as sweeping across south-eastern Russia like some elemental catastrophe. The rebellion is led by Emelyan Pugachov, who first appears to the narrator and his driver in the middle of a snow-storm, as if born from it; for a moment, they are unsure whether he is man or wolf.

All three works spring from the fifty-six short lines of one of Pushkin's most remarkable lyrics. The language of 'Demons' is colloquial; the whirling trochaic rhythm mimics the whirl of the blizzard in which the speaker and his driver are lost; verbs of motion – 'rush', 'weave', 'drive', 'whirl' – are repeated insistently. The presence of supernatural forces goes unquestioned. Near the beginning of the poem, the driver explains that the horses are being led astray by a demon. By the end of the poem the whirling snowflakes have become swarms of demons, and they may be performing some ritual: perhaps a witch's wedding, or the burial of a house spirit. Like Shakespeare, Pushkin is a profoundly popular poet; he writes not as an aristocrat taking an interest in the language and beliefs of the peasantry, but as if from the heart of their world. Here he seems to be writing as if from the heart of nature itself. The poem is a shamanic vision; it is, perhaps, a vision of evil, but the tone is oddly neutral. Like a shaman, Pushkin simply tells what he sees and hears; in the last line we learn that the sounds he hears 'rend his heart', but even this is reported coolly and objectively.

There is a similar impersonality about the evocations of violence in *The Captain's Daughter*. Pushkin does, once, famously, voice his feelings about this violence – in the often quoted words 'God spare us from Russian revolt, senseless merciless Russian revolt' – but for the main part he accepts it as a given. The depth of understanding behind his 'archaic smile' seems to lend him the power not only to foreshadow the course of Russian literature but also to predict the catastrophes of Russian history.

Eugene Onegin
1823–31

The house is full; the boxes brilliant;
Parterre and stalls – all seethe and roar;
Up in the gods they clap, ebullient,
And, with a swish, the curtains soar.
Semi-ethereal and radiant,
To the enchanting bow obedient,
Ringed round by nymphs, Istómina
Stands still; one foot supporting her,
She circles slowly with the other,
And lo! a leap, and lo! she flies,
Flies off like fluff across the skies,
By Aeolus wafted hither thither;
Her waist she twists, untwists; her feet
Against each other swiftly beat.

Eugene Onegin, I, 20

Pushkin has sometimes seemed in danger of being buried beneath a crushing weight of reverence. As early as 1834, two years before the poet's death, Gogol wrote that Pushkin was 'perhaps the only manifestation of the Russian spirit [...] the Russian [...] as he perhaps will appear in 200 years'. In a famous speech given at the unveiling in 1880 of a statue to Pushkin, Dostoevsky claimed that Pushkin was a 'unique and unprecedented phenomenon' in world literature, a 'diviner and prophet' of Russia's future messianic role in European history. And the 10th February 1937 front-page editorial of *Pravda* (the Communist Party newspaper) began: 'A hundred years have passed since the greatest Russian poet, Alexander Sergeyevich Pushkin, was shot by the hand of a foreign aristocratic scoundrel, a hireling of Tsarism.' The editorial continued: 'Pushkin's creation merged with the October socialist revolution as a river flows into the ocean.'[11]

Gogol, Dostoevsky, the anonymous editorial-writer – and thousands like them – have lost sight of Pushkin and his individuality. Instead, Gogol sees him as the embodiment of 'the Russian spirit'; Dostoevsky sees him as the embodiment of 'the all-human and all-uniting Russian soul'; and the editorial-writer sees him as the embodiment of Sovietness. There have, of course, always been writers who have tried to save Pushkin from the cult that has grown around him. Two of the most important of these are Vladimir Nabokov and Andrey Sinyavsky, both of whom ended their lives as exiles. Sinyavsky writes, 'Lightness is the first thing we get out of his works [...] Before Pushkin there was almost no light verse [in Russia...] And suddenly, out of the blue – curtsies and turns comparable to nothing and no one, speed, momentum, bounciness, the ability to prance, to gallop, to take hurdles, to do the splits [...]'[12] Pushkin, in Sinyavsky's view, is a dancer – like the ballerina Pushkin describes in the stanza above from *Eugene Onegin*.

The 'Onegin stanza' – the set of rules that allows Pushkin to dance – is Pushkin's own creation. It is typical of Pushkin to have called *Eugene Onegin* 'a novel in verse', thus asserting his freedom from conventional genres, yet to have chosen for his free-flowing novel an unusually tight and demanding stanza form. Each stanza is made up of fourteen lines, and each line of four iambic feet. The rhyme scheme can be described as aBaBccDDeFFeGG; the lowercase letters represent feminine rhymes (stressed on the penultimate syllable), and the uppercase – masculine rhymes (stressed on the final syllable). Nabokov has famously compared the opening quatrain and the final couplet to 'patterns on a painted ball or top that are visible at the beginning and at the end of the spin'. He goes on to say that 'the main spinning process' involves lines five to twelve, 'where a fluent and variable phrasing blurs the contours of the lines so that they are seldom seen as clearly consisting of two couplets and a closed quatrain'.[13]

Pushkin began *Eugene Onegin* on 9th May 1823 and completed the main body of the poem on 25th September 1830 in Boldino; he added Onegin's letter to Tatiana in August 1831. A complete edition was first published in 1833. The poem is a perfect unity, even though the tone changes from chapter to chapter. Mirsky has written that:

> *Eugene Onegin* is like a living growth: the same throughout, and yet different. We recognise in the eighth chapter the style of the first as we recognise a familiar face, changed by age. The difference is great and yet the essential proportions are the same. It is a face of unique beauty.

The plot, as always with Pushkin, is simple. A bored, Byronic man about town, Eugene Onegin, retires to the country. There he befriends a young neighbour, Vladimir Lensky, a Romantic poet who is in love with a local girl, Olga Larina. Olga's elder sister, Tatiana, falls in love with Onegin; she confesses her love in a long letter. Onegin tells her that he is too disillusioned with life to be capable of love. On Tatiana's name-day, Onegin flirts with Olga. Lensky challenges him to a duel; Onegin kills him. Onegin goes on a long journey. Three years later Onegin meets Tatiana once again; she is now a St Petersburg *grande dame*, the wife of a general. Onegin writes her a love letter – a mirror image of hers to him. She says she still loves him, but that she will remain faithful to her husband.

The mid-nineteenth-century radical critic Vissarion Belinsky famously referred to *Onegin* as 'an encyclopaedia of Russian life'.

Pushkin's poem-novel is indeed all-inclusive; it is hard to describe it except through paradoxes. Its sparkling levity proves able to incorporate tragedy, and the simple plot has room for the wildest, most inconsequential digressions. For all the artifice, there is a density of realistic detail that has led some critics to see *Onegin* as the beginning of Russian realism. And for all the realistic detail, there is a delight in sound and rhythm, a high-spirited playfulness, that has led others to see Pushkin as a believer in 'art for art's sake'. Pushkin is often at his most 'literary' when describing details of everyday life – and at his most realistic when showing how his characters model themselves, with disastrous results, on the heroes and heroines of fashionable books they have read. And he resolves the linguistic controversies of the time by assert- ing – often through making a mock apology – his right to employ *every* kind of vocabulary: simple Russian, archaic Russian, Church Slavonicisms, or borrowings from French, German and English. Few novels embody more of the openness of real life. *Onegin* repeatedly surprises the reader, and it clearly retained the capacity to surprise Pushkin himself. In an often quoted letter he wrote, 'My Tatiana has gone and got married! I should never have thought it of her.'

For all the hypocritical attempts of politicians and ideologues to enlist Pushkin to their cause, there have always been many people who have felt that Pushkin embodies something deeply precious; this 'something' can perhaps best be defined as 'grace' – and none of Pushkin's works is imbued with more of this grace than *Eugene Onegin*. In a speech at the Petrograd House of Writers in 1921, on the eighty-fourth anniversary of Pushkin's death, the poet Vladislav Khodasevich (who was soon to emig- rate) talked of how the 'Pushkinian sun' would soon be eclipsed. He ended: 'our desire to make the day of Pushkin's death a day of universal remembrance is, I think, partly prompted by this same premonition: we are coming to an agreement about how to call out to one another, by what name to hail one another in the impending darkness.'[14]

Loyal subject and family man
1831–3

> Let not a poet's soul be frozen,
> Made rough and hard, reduced to bone
> And finally be turned to stone
> In that benumbing world he goes in,
> In that intoxicating slough
> Where, friends, we bathe together now.
>
> *Eugene Onegin*, VI, 46

In 1826, four years before his marriage, Pushkin's life appeared to have been transformed. The Tsar had pardoned him; he was at the height of his popularity; and he had no idea of the difficulties he would face with Benckendorff. At the beginning of the 1830s, immediately before and after his marriage, Pushkin was once again trying to establish himself in the world, to put his life on a firmer footing; this time, however, he was well aware that this could be done only through hard work and painful compromise. One of the compromises he needed to make was with regard to his *Comedy*. Publication – and, better still, performance – could earn him money, bolster his reputation and, perhaps, improve his now deteriorating relationship with the Tsar.

During 1827 and 1828 Pushkin had managed to publish several scenes from the play in journals. He had also continued to give readings to private audiences until receiving another reprimand from Benckendorff in June 1828. Praise for the play had continued to grow – not only among Russians. The great Polish poet Adam Mickiewicz (whom Pushkin had met both in Moscow and St Petersburg) had compared Pushkin to Shakespeare, and the January 1829 issue of the London-published *Foreign Quarterly Review* had hailed the play as the beginning of 'a new era in Russian dramatic literature'.

In 1829 Pushkin had asked Zhukovsky – whom the Tsar trusted, and whom he had appointed in 1826 as tutor to his son, the future Alexander II – to take responsibility for some small changes to the text in an attempt to get it past the censorship. The changes, however, were too slight, and Nicholas once again refused. Benckendorff was oddly slow to let Pushkin know of this.

Later in 1829 Pushkin learned that Benckendorff was in cahoots with Pushkin's most influential literary enemy, Faddey Bulgarin. Bulgarin was a police informer, a bad writer with an inflated view of himself, and the editor of the patriotic newspaper *The Northern Bee*. Benckendorff had shown Pushkin's manuscript to Bulgarin, and Bulgarin had plagiarised from it for a dull historical novel of his own that was published in February 1830. Pushkin's Lycée friend Anton Delvig printed a hostile review in *The Literary Gazette*, a short-lived journal that he and Pushkin co-edited throughout 1830. Bulgarin wrote a vicious reply and throughout that year *The Literary Gazette* and *The Northern Bee* traded insults.

Bulgarin claimed to have the Tsar's patronage, but this was a lie. In reality, his patron was Benckendorff; the Tsar merely tolerated him. The Tsar sometimes gave books by Pushkin and Zhukovsky as gifts; he never gave books by Bulgarin. When Bulgarin overreached himself, when he began attacking Zhukovsky as well as Pushkin and Delvig, the Tsar intimated to Zhukovsky that Pushkin should apply again for permission to publish his *Comedy*. Pushkin did this, and the Tsar granted his permission in late April – though it seemed that the play would still have to be submitted to the regular censorship.

The July 1830 revolution in France alarmed the Russian authorities and made the censors more vigilant than ever. Determined to outmanoeuvre Bulgarin, Pushkin cut from his play anything that could be seen as provocative or pro-Polish. He also decided to dedicate the play to the memory of Nikolai Karamzin – Russia's first *historiograph* or 'Historian Laureate' and the embodiment of political orthodoxy.

Meanwhile the political stakes grew only higher. Inspired by the revolution in France, the Poles rebelled against Russian rule in November. Pushkin's politically sanitised version of *Boris Godunov* was published in January 1831, just as Russia was preparing to invade Poland. The Tsar informed Pushkin, through Benckendorff, that he had read *Boris Godunov* 'with especial pleasure'. And Smirdin – the St Petersburg bookseller – bought the entire print run, probably of 2,400 copies, paying Pushkin 10,000 roubles as well as reimbursing Pletnyov for the costs of production.

Poland asked France for support; Pushkin seems to have been deeply concerned that French intervention might start a new European war. France, however, did nothing, and in late August 1831, the Russian army entered Warsaw. Pushkin and Zhukovsky published a joint brochure, *On the Taking of Warsaw*. This contained one poem by Zhukovsky and two by Pushkin: 'Borodino Anniversary' and 'To the Slanderers of Russia'. The last and most important of these three poems is addressed primarily to a group of French politicians who had been critical of Russia. Pushkin's central argument is one that was to be repeated more than once by the Soviet regime: that this was a quarrel between Slavs, a 'domestic quarrel', and that it was not for outsiders to interfere. Many liberals, including Vyazemsky, accused Pushkin of toadying to the Tsar; this was almost certainly unfair. Pushkin was probably delighted by the chance to write a public, political poem in which he could show his loyalty to the Tsar – but this does not mean that his nationalism was insincere; even as a young radical, after all, he had been supportive of Russian imperialism in the Caucasus.

The Tsar was quick to show his gratitude. The three poems were presented to him on 3rd September. The brochure was published on 11th September. And on 14th September Alexander Turgenev heard rumours that Pushkin was being appointed 'Historian Laureate'. This was a great honour. No one except Karamzin had held this title before, and history and literature were at this time seen as one and the same thing; the title was thus an official recognition of Pushkin's status as Russia's leading writer. The title also brought unrestricted access to State historical archives. The importance of this cannot be overestimated; Pushkin's greatest ambition during his last years was to write a *History of Peter the Great*.

Pushkin was not a Romantic 'half in love with easeful Death'. In the breadth of his interests, and in his determination to be a man of the world, he has more in common with Goethe than with any of the English Romantics. The readiness to compromise which he showed around the time of his marriage testifies to the strength of his wish to live a saner, more complete and more integrated life. Curiously, the sacrifices he made are all linked by a common thread. To be a good husband, he had to banish thoughts of the Polish Karolina Sobańska; to get his *Comedy* published, he had to excise from it any elements that could be seen as pro-Polish; to become Historian Laureate, he had to defend the Russian invasion of Poland. Lastly, his enemy, Bulgarin, was of Polish origin. In a letter of December 1830, Pushkin wrote that he hoped that the coming war against Poland would be 'a war of extermination'. It is possible that, at some deeper level in his mind, he might have meant 'a war against all elements that might threaten his new position in the world' – but these are dangerous words, no matter how one interprets them. 'A war of extermination' – whether it is being fought against another country or against a part of oneself – always demands of its perpetrators a higher price than they expect.

Pushkin was always attracted to extreme action and the chauvinist elements in him cannot be wished away. He did not repeat his call for the Poles to be exterminated, but he remained proud of his anti-Polish poems until his last days.

Pushkin and his wife seem to have been happy during the first weeks of their marriage – though Pushkin seems to have sensed this happiness as fragile. In a letter to Pletnyov a week after their wedding he wrote, 'I am married – and happy; my only desire is that nothing in my life should change – I can expect nothing better. This state is so new to me that I seem to have been born again.' Pushkin and Natalya led a busy social life, and there are several accounts of their appearing at social events, looking happy and contented together.

Natalya's mother, however, seems to have continued to criticise Pushkin to his wife. Within five weeks Pushkin had made up his mind to spend the summer and autumn in Tsarskoye Selo. He and Natalya left Moscow in mid-May. A month later, Pushkin wrote a furious letter to Natalya's mother, but Natalya was able to persuade him not to send it; his wife may have been thirteen years younger than him, but Pushkin was evidently able to listen to her.

In July the court arrived in Tsarskoye Selo; the cholera epidemic that had kept Pushkin in Boldino had now spread further north and forced the Court to leave St Petersburg. This interrupted the 'inspirational solitude' Pushkin had hoped for, but it brought him the pleasure of seeing Zhukovsky almost every day. The two poets often paid joint visits to Alexandra Rosset, an intelligent and beautiful lady in waiting whom Pushkin admired and to whom Zhukovsky had once proposed. Zhukovsky wrote a great deal during these months, including the 'Tale of Tsar Berendey'. In friendly rivalry, Pushkin wrote the finest of his own verse fairy-tales, 'The Tale of Tsar Saltan'. The young Nikolai Gogol, who was staying nearby, in Pavlovsk, wrote ecstatically to a friend about hearing the two poets read their 'completely Russian' work.

Natalya, for her part, seems to have quickly established herself in her new role. She was soon presented to the Empress and, when the Pushkins moved in October to St Petersburg, she was an immediate social success there. She soon became a favourite of the Tsar, an acknowledged beauty who was invited to all the most important balls. She was fortunate to have an aunt, Yekaterina Zagryazhskaya, who had been a lady in waiting for twenty-five years. Zagryazhskaya guided Natalya through the intricacies of court etiquette, provided her with most of her ball gowns and helped with other expenses. Pushkin liked her and was grateful for her help. Over the years, however, she would consistently oppose him on one important question: that of a possible move to the country. Thinking that life in the country would be cheaper, and that it would leave him more time to write, Pushkin was to try several times to leave St Petersburg. Zagryazhskaya saw this as unthinkable: Natalya – in her view – was someone born to shine in society.

In a letter of October 1831 to his old friend and fellow gambler Pavel Nashchokin, Pushkin wrote, 'Marrying, I thought I'd be spending three times as much as before – but it turns out to be ten times.' From autumn 1831, Pushkin's financial problems never ceased to compound. For the rest of his life he was borrowing more and more money – from friends, from acquaintances, from professional moneylenders, even from the Tsar. He ran up debts with tradespeople of all kinds. He tried hard to increase his income but was unable to control his expenses; by the time of his death, his debts amounted to about 140,000 roubles – a vast sum in relation to his government salary of 5,000 roubles a year, or to the 12,000 roubles he earned in March 1833 from one of his most lucrative books – the first complete edition of *Eugene Onegin*. The heavily mortgaged family estates provided less than his government salary; having been badly run in the past, they also often proved an administrative burden.

Pushkin never completely stopped gambling, but gambling was no longer the main cause of his debts; they went on increasing simply because he could never earn enough to support the grand life that he and his wife were leading. He was also often called upon to bail out his own and his wife's relatives; his younger brother, Lev, seems to have been particularly irresponsible.

In his letters Pushkin frequently makes anxious references to these debts; as often as not, he is simply planning to borrow from one person in order to pay off another. These passages make depressing reading, and Binyon's detailed analyses are still more depressing. Pushkin's financial situation was deeply troubling; it was, no doubt, one of the reasons for the outbursts of self-destructive behaviour that were to grow ever more frequent during his last years.

A first child, Maria, was born to the Pushkins in May 1832. In a letter to Vera Vyazemskaya (Prince Vyazemsky's wife, who had been a close friend and confidante to Pushkin since his last months in Odessa), Pushkin wrote, 'Just imagine, my wife has had the maladroitness to give birth to a little lithograph of me. I am in despair, for all my vanity.' Their first son, Alexander, would be born in July 1833; Maria and Alexander would be followed by Grigory (1835) and Natalya (1836).

During December 1831, while Natalya was halfway through her first pregnancy, Pushkin had spent three weeks in Moscow. The letters he wrote to Natalya at that time are affectionate but also somewhat anxious. Pushkin seems uncertain whether his young wife will be able to cope with managing the household. His letters to her during a second absence in September 1832 are a little different in tone. They are still anxiously affectionate, but the focus of the anxieties has changed. His concern now is not that Natalya may be unable to manage, but that she may be extravagant. And he has become obsessed with her flirting. In letter after letter he either admonishes her not to flirt with particular men – ranging from his friend, Sergei Sobolevsky, to Tsar Nicholas – or else, with half-joking magnanimity, he gives her his permission to flirt with them. However justified his anxieties, it is also likely that he was projecting onto Natalya repressed promiscuous desires of his own.

Natalya continued to attract admiration. On 8th February 1833 the Emperor declared Natalya the 'Queen' of a very grand masquerade ball; Natalya had dressed as the Priestess of the Sun. Pushkin continued to feel oppressed by his debts and by the demands on his time. In a letter to Nashchokin he wrote, 'Worries about life keep me from boredom. But I do not have leisure, that free bachelor life necessary for the writer. I whirl about in society, my wife is in high fashion – all this demands money, I obtain money through labours, and labours demand solitude.' Gogol and Pletnyov both wrote critically, in letters, about Pushkin frittering away his life going to balls; neither seems to have realised that he may not have been doing this entirely by choice. A positive element in Pushkin's life was that he remained on good terms with the Tsar. At a ball at the Austrian Embassy in February 1833, the Tsar talked to Pushkin for some time about his work on Peter the Great; Pushkin was generally understood to be a favourite.

In late 1832 Pushkin had begun *Dubrovsky*, an adventure novel that he never completed. One of his reasons for abandoning it was his increasing interest in the Pugachov rebellion – a major uprising, in the early 1770s, of Cossacks, peasants and non-Russian tribespeople. In 1824 Pushkin had referred to Stenka Razin (Russia's other great peasant rebel) as the 'most poetic figure in Russian history'; and in 1826, as Maria Volkonskaya was about to travel to Siberia to join her Decembrist husband, Pushkin had told her that he wanted to write 'a work about Pugachov'. In January 1833, after writing an outline of what would later become *The Captain's Daughter* – a historical novel set against the background of this rebellion – Pushkin obtained permission to carry out research on Pugachov in the state archives. He then decided to write not a novel but a work of historical research. Between 25th February and 8th March, he read over a thousand pages of documents, summarising some and copying down others in full. During April and May he wrote a first draft of *A History of Pugachov*. In August, wanting to speak to eyewitnesses, he travelled to south-eastern Russia, to Kazan, Orenburg and the Urals. In a letter to his wife he wrote about meeting a former mistress of Pugachov's:

> In the village of Berdy, where Pugachov was encamped for six months, I had *une bonne fortune* – I found a 75-year-old Cossack woman who remembers that time as well as you and I remember 1830. I went on and on pestering her, and I didn't even think of you – I'm sorry. Now I hope to get a lot of things into order, get a lot written, and then come to you with the booty.

This Cossack woman, who had been one of Pugachov's concubines, also sang three songs about Pugachov and showed Pushkin the hut where Pugachov had lived. On his way back from the south-east, in early October, he stopped at Boldino and – amongst much else – completed a second draft of *Pugachov*.

On 25th November he returned to St Petersburg. Zhukovsky had come back two months before him, after spending over a year in Germany. Once more Pushkin was able to attend the regular literary Saturdays Zhukovsky held in his apartment.

And, on 12th December, Pushkin had a meeting with Benckendorff. Pushkin had submitted *The Bronze Horseman* to him a week before this, and Benckendorff wished to give the poem back to him with the Tsar's comments. The Tsar had crossed out four lines and inserted a number of question marks. Pushkin clearly found it difficult to comply with these criticisms. At first he did nothing; in 1836 he tried to revise the poem but gave up. However much he needed to earn money, some compromises seem to have been beyond him. *The Bronze Horseman* was first published only after Pushkin's death – in a version that Zhukovsky had edited, and seriously distorted, to meet the Tsar's wishes.

Return to Boldino
Autumn 1833

Melancholy time, enchantment of the eyes.

Pushkin, 'Autumn', 1833

Pushkin's second autumn in Boldino was still more fruitful than his stay there in the autumn of 1830, shortly before his marriage. During this second stay he not only completed *Pugachov* but also wrote 'Andzhelo' (a narrative poem distilled from Shakespeare's *Measure for Measure*), two verse fairy tales and two of his masterpieces, *The Bronze Horseman* and *The Queen of Spades*.

We are fortunate to have several accounts of Pushkin during this autumn, from different viewpoints. We have the report of a government informer: 'The aforesaid Pushkin [...] during the whole time of his sojourn occupied himself exclusively only with composition alone [sic], he called on none of his neighbours and received no one.' From a letter to his wife, we can see Pushkin as he believed he was seen by his neighbours:

Do you know what people nearby are saying about me? Here's how they describe my activities: 'When Pushkin writes poetry, he has a decanter of the finest liqueur standing in front of him. He downs one glass, a second, a third – and then he gets writing!' There's fame for you!

And we have Pushkin's own account of his activities – also from a letter to his wife:

I wake at seven o'clock; I drink coffee, and I lie around until three o'clock. Not long ago I got into a writing vein and I've written a mass of stuff. At three o'clock I mount my horse, at five, I take a bath, and then I dine on potatoes and buckwheat porridge. I read until nine o'clock. There's my day for you. And they're all just the same.

It should be added that Pushkin often composed while lying in bed, his manuscript propped on his knees; this is what he means by 'lying around'.

Pushkin's words tally with the informer's report. Nevertheless, but for the claim to have 'written a mass of stuff', it would be hard to guess from this letter, or from Pushkin's other letters to Natalya from Boldino, that he was being visited by inspiration. At least half of these letters are taken up by money worries, and Pushkin seems more obsessed than ever with his wife's flirting. Earlier in this letter of 30th October, for example, he writes:

Look here: it's not for nothing that flirting is out of fashion and is considered a sign of bad *ton*. There's little sense in it. You rejoice that male dogs are running after you, as after a little bitch, raising their tails like pokers and sniffing you in the arse. Is that really something to rejoice over?

In subsequent letters Pushkin half apologises for his rudeness, but he proves unable to keep off this subject.

One more glimpse of Pushkin at this time is provided by 'Autumn', an autobiographical poem of eighty-nine lines in which he expresses his delight in this season. The prose meaning of the last four stanzas is as follows:

And every autumn I blossom anew; the Russian cold is good for my health; once again I feel love for the habits of everyday life. Sleep comes at its proper time, as does hunger; the blood plays lightly and joyfully in my heart; desires seethe. Again I am happy and young, again I am full of life – such is my organism (excuse this uncalled-for prosaicism).

They bring me a horse; shaking its mane, it carries its rider through wide-open spaces, and the frozen valley rings out beneath its sparkling hoof, and the ice cracks. But the short day fades, and fire burns again in the forgotten fireplace, now pouring out bright light, now slowly smouldering; I read in front of it, or nourish long thoughts in my soul.

And I forget the world – and in sweet silence am sweetly lulled by my imagination, and poetry awakens in me; my soul is gripped by lyric agitation, it trembles, sounds, and seeks, as in a dream, to pour itself out at last in free manifestation; and then an invisible swarm of guests comes towards me – old familiars, fruits of my own dreaming.

And thoughts stir boldly in my head, and light rhymes run to meet them, and fingers beg for a pen, pen for paper; another minute – and verses will flow freely. So a ship dozes motionless in motionless water; but look – suddenly the sailors all rush about, climb up and down, and the sails swell, filled with the wind, and the vast bulk moves forward and cuts the waves apart.

Off it sails. Where then shall we sail?

During his stay in Boldino, Pushkin sailed in his imagination to many places – but his two most important journeys were back to St Petersburg. In *The Queen of Spades* we glimpse the St Petersburg of Catherine the Great. In his pursuit of a gambler's secret that will guarantee him a fortune, the hero, Hermann, treats two women – the old Countess and the young Lizaveta Ivanovna – with absolute ruthlessness. He himself is in the grip of dark forces over which he has no control. How we understand these forces is unimportant; what matters is that, having abandoned both religious faith and moral values, Hermann has no protection against them. The story ends tragically; Hermann unwittingly brings about the death of the Countess and then goes mad himself.

In *The Bronze Horseman* we see the St Petersburg of two other epochs. The poem's introduction begins with an account of Peter the Great standing in the desolate marshes of the Gulf of Finland and deciding to build a city there, 'to break open a window into Europe'. This leads into a panegyric to the beauty and grandeur of St Petersburg as it was in Pushkin's day. Parts One and Two of the poem are set at the time of the flood of November 1824. There are two central characters: a minor civil servant by the name of Yevgeny; and Peter the Great, in the guise of the 'Bronze Horseman' – the famous equestrian statue commissioned by Catherine the Great.

Part One focuses on Yevgeny's dreams of independence and marriage. His beloved, Parasha, lives with her mother on Vasilevsky Island; he himself lives on the mainland. The storm makes it impossible to cross the Neva for several days, and the young couple are unable to meet; then the river bursts its banks in the worst flood since the city was founded. Desperately anxious about Parasha, Yevgeny finds shelter near the Bronze Horseman; he sits down on a marble lion by the entrance to a new palace.

In Part Two, Yevgeny crosses the river as the flood begins to subside. Seeing no trace of Parasha's house, he loses his mind. A year later he is once again standing beside the Bronze Horseman. Blaming Peter for founding the city beside the sea, he utters a vague threat. The Bronze Horseman appears to respond angrily. Yevgeny runs away; the Horseman gallops after him. Soon afterwards Yevgeny dies. His corpse is found where Parasha's house had once stood.

The poem is usually seen as a study of the conflict between the rights of the individual and the claims of historical necessity.

It has been said that Pushkin remains neutral in regard to this conflict; it would be truer to say that he sympathises passionately with both sides. Pushkin sincerely admired Peter the Great throughout his life. His assertion of Russia's 'historical destiny' is also, in part, a retort to Adam Mickiewicz. Upset by Pushkin's and Zhukovsky's *The Taking of Warsaw*, the Polish poet had accused the two Russians of sycophancy. Pushkin's indignant retort is that it is as futile for the Poles to rebel against Moscow as for Yevgeny to threaten the Bronze Horseman.

Pushkin's sympathy for Yevgeny is equally real. Like Yevgeny, Pushkin felt persecuted and powerless. His moving and sombre short poem 'God grant that I do not go mad' was written during this same stay in Boldino – as, of course, was the description of Hermann's madness in *The Queen of Spades*.

The Bronze Horseman has continued to excite controversy. Anatol Lunacharsky, the first Bolshevik Commissar for Enlightenment, insisted that Pushkin's sympathies were on the side of Peter the Great. In an article written for the centenary of Pushkin's death in 1937, the great Soviet prose writer Andrey Platonov replied that the everyday values represented by Yevgeny, the 'little man', matter no less than the values embodied by the Bronze Horseman. Without Yevgeny and people like him – Platonov wrote – we would be left with 'nothing but bronze [...] and the Admiralty spire would turn into a candlestick beside the coffin of the dead (or destroyed) poetic human soul'.

In both *The Queen of Spades* and *The Bronze Horseman* human life is seen as fragile and delicate. In *The Bronze Horseman* it is at the mercy both of the elements and of the bronze might of emperors. In *The Queen of Spades* people are constantly in danger of turning into stone, into automata. By the end of the story Hermann's soul has turned to stone and the Countess, whose soul had long ago turned to stone, is dead. What will become of Lizaveta Ivanovna is unknown. She may follow the example of the old Countess; or the quivering flame of the 'poetic human soul' may continue to live in her.

Pushkin and History
1825–37

The history of the people belongs to the poet.

Letter from Pushkin to Gnedich, the Russian translator of Homer,
23rd February 1825

Pushkin was both Russia's greatest poet and one of her first great historians. Unlike Karamzin's work, Pushkin's still seems fresh and modern. In 1830 Pushkin wrote that it is not for the dramatic poet to 'excuse, condemn or prompt', that authentic tragedy must be 'as impartial as Fate', and that this impartiality can be achieved only if the playwright resolves 'to express the people of the past, their minds, their prejudices' according to the value system of their time rather than that of his own time. Pushkin admired Walter Scott – who was widely read in Russia in the 1830s – but he wrote more succinctly than Scott and his goal was more serious; he wanted to know about the past not in order to escape from the present but in order to understand it. And he was not content merely to admire the past from a distance; when making a copy for himself of one of Peter the Great's letters, he imitated his handwriting – as if hoping that this would help him to enter into Peter's heart and mind.

Pushkin's interest in history goes back a long way. During his last years in the Lycée, he was a regular visitor to the home of the historian Nikolai Karamzin; in 1816 he even lived there for several months. As a young man in St Petersburg, he was excited by his first reading of Karamzin's *History of the Russian State*. And he wrote his first serious historical article, 'Notes on Eighteenth-Century Russian History', as early as 1822. This article, unpublished in Pushkin's lifetime, is full of such tersely expressed insights as 'If to rule means to know the weakness of the human soul and how to exploit it, then Catherine deserves the astonished admiration of posterity.'

Two years after this, in Odessa, Pushkin was able to do his first serious research from original sources. Count Vorontsov had a fine library that included letters sent to one of his relatives by Alexander Radishchev, a Russian radical thinker whom Catherine the Great exiled to Siberia, together with her comments on his banned *Journey from St Petersburg to Moscow*. Pushkin was to publish an article about Radishchev twelve years later, in *The Contemporary*; he also mentioned him, respectfully, in an early draft of one of his last poems, *'Exegi monumentum'*.

As we have seen, Pushkin's play *The Comedy of Tsar Boris and Grishka Otrepyev* (1825) has been undervalued both as history and as drama. Whether in the nineteenth or the twentieth century, it has been at least as hard to be a good historian in Russia as to be a good poet. In the end, Pushkin was obliged to castrate his *Comedy*. It is ironic that it was in order to become 'Historian Laureate' that Pushkin was obliged to betray the truer historical understanding it embodies. The *Comedy* is livelier than *Boris Godunov* in every way – with more variety of tone, metre and subject matter – but it is only during the last decade that this earlier version has begun to re-emerge.

From the mid-1820s Pushkin had been collecting material about Peter the Great and his times, and during his last years he was working on a monograph about him that he hoped would be his chef-d'oeuvre; it is tragic that he died without finishing it. Peter the Great does, however, appear in several of Pushkin's creative works: the unfinished novel *The Blackamoor of Peter the Great*, and the verse narratives *Poltava* and *The Bronze Horseman*.

The Blackamoor of Peter the Great is important as Pushkin's first attempt at narrative prose. *Poltava* is important as part of Pushkin's continuing project to fuse poetry and history. The poem is centred on the battle of Poltava (1709), Peter the Great's crucial victory in the Great Northern War against Sweden; it ends with an epilogue in praise of Peter the Great. And just as *Boris Godunov* inspired an opera by Mussorgsky, so *Poltava* inspired an opera by Tchaikovsky: *Mazeppa*.

The failings of both *The Blackamoor* and *Poltava* may stem from Pushkin's inability, at the time, to find the right perspective from which to view Peter the Great. A memoir by the lexicographer Vladimir Dahl suggests that this may have been what Pushkin himself thought. Dahl remembers him saying of Peter the Great:

> I still cannot understand that giant and comprehend him with my mind: he is too huge for us short-sighted ones, and we are still too close to him […] but I understand him with my heart; the longer I study him, the more astonishment and reverence deprive me of the means of thinking and judging freely. […] But I will make something out of this gold. O, you will see: I will yet accomplish much.

This conversation took place in September 1833, when Dahl was showing Pushkin around Orenburg and other towns and villages associated with Pugachov; only six weeks later, in *The Bronze Horseman*, Pushkin was to portray Peter, with total assurance, from a variety of unexpected and revealing perspectives.

Pushkin's one completed work of pure history was *The History of Pugachov*. This was published in December 1834, in two volumes: the first was Pushkin's narrative, the second a collection of source materials. Pushkin also wrote some confidential notes for the Tsar alone. These are startlingly forthright:

All the common people were with Pugachov. The clergy sympathised – not only village priests and monks but even archimandrites and bishops. Only the nobility was openly on the side of the government. [...] If we analyse the measures taken by Pugachov and his comrades, we must admit that they chose the most reliable and effective means of achieving their goals. The government, in contrast, acted weakly, slowly and mistakenly.

Even in the published volumes Pushkin is almost as critical of the Russian military leadership.

A History of Pugachov is an extraordinary work, unlike any other historical work of its time. It is based on archival research and first-hand interviews, and Pushkin makes no attempt to impose any false coherence on the chaos of events. The number of accounts of minor battles and random movements of small detachments of troops is dizzying. It is hard to imagine that even Pushkin himself could have held all the details of the campaigns in his mind. Instead of frustrating the reader, however, this has the effect of reinforcing his trust in Pushkin's honesty. In any case, Pushkin has already forestalled criticism by including, as an epigraph, some sentences by a cleric who had already written about the rebellion:

To render a proper account of all the designs and adventures of this impostor would, it seems, be almost impossible [...] because all of this impostor's undertakings depended, not on rational considerations or military precepts, but on daring, happenstance and luck. For this reason (I think) Pugachov himself would not only be unable to recount all the details of these undertakings, but would not even be aware of a considerable portion of them, since they were initiated, not just by him directly, but by many of his unbridled daredevil accomplices in several locations at once.

Just as individual characters in *The Captain's Daughter* anticipate individual characters in Tolstoy's works, so Pushkin's own thoughts anticipate the whole of Tolstoy's philosophy of history – both in this epigraph and in *The History of Pugachov* as a whole.

Against this chaotic background, individual characters and voices stand out poignantly. The experience of reading the book is like being carried through rapids and occasionally glimpsing a person on the bank or hearing their voice. Sometimes these voices are the voices of folk poetry, and they ring out with startling vividness:

Soon the spring thaw set in; the rivers began to flow again and the bodies of those killed at Tatishchev began to float past the fortresses. Wives and mothers stood by the bank, trying to recognise their husbands and sons. One old Cossack woman used to wander along the Yaik near Ozernaya every day, drawing the floating corpses to the bank with a walking stick and saying again and again, 'Is that not you, my child? Is that not you my Stepushka? Are those not your black curls being washed by the fresh water?' Seeing a face she did not know, she would gently push the corpse away.

Even in this predominantly factual work Pushkin remains, as ever, a poet – and he shows a constant awareness of the importance of language. He criticises the 'tangled and obscure style' of a manifesto about Pugachov published by Reinsdorp, the governor of Orenburg. And in his 'Notes' for the Tsar, Pushkin wrote: 'Pugachov's first seditious appeal to the Yaik Cossacks is an astonishing example of popular eloquence, for all its faults of grammar. It was all the more effective given that Reinsdorp's announcements, or rather publications, were written in a style as feeble as it was correct.'

A contemporary reviewer of *Pugachov* regretted that it had been 'painted in a limp, cold and dry fashion, and not with the fiery brush of a Byron'. Baron Rozen, a friend of Pushkin, wrote in reply:

> That our great poet was able not to be a poet in his History
> [...] demonstrates how well he understands the immutable
> bounds of each of the fine arts. [...] A sage economy in and
> an elegant arrangement of material; a precise, genuinely
> artistic chiaroscuro, and, finally an inimitable concision of
> style, in which not a single redundant epithet can be found,
> – all this is gratifying proof of a great historical talent.[15]

Everything Rozen says is true – except that Pushkin *is* a poet in his *Pugachov*, if of an unusual kind.

Junior Gentleman of the Chamber
1834–6

Enough, my friend, it's time. The heart asks peace;
Day after day flies past, and every hour
Makes off with some small particle of being.
Pushkin, 'It's time, my friend', 1834

In a diary entry for 1st January 1834 Pushkin wrote:

The day before yesterday I was appointed a *kammerjunker*
(which is somewhat unbecoming to my years). But the
Court wanted Natalya Nikolaevna to dance at the Anichkov
Palace. I am content, because the sovereign wished to distinguish me, not to make me absurd. As far as I'm concerned, they can make me a page – just as long as I don't
have to study French vowels and arithmetic...

The title of *kammerjunker* ('junior gentleman of the chamber')
was usually conferred on high aristocrats in their mid-twenties,
and it is understandable that Pushkin should have felt humiliated.
He was afraid that he would look ridiculous beside the other,
younger *kammerjunkers*. He was aware that he had been awarded
the title at least partly in order to make it easier for Nicholas
to invite Natalya to royal balls. He was also concerned that being
seen as a court lackey would discredit him as a national poet.
For all these reasons, Pushkin was furious. In his diary entry for

17th January, after a ball during which he had spoken to Nicholas for the first time since this appointment, he wrote, 'the sovereign did not speak to me about my appointment as a *kammerjunker*, and I did not thank him.'

Natalya, on the other hand, may well have been delighted by her husband's new title. Her official presentation at court was a great success and at one important ball in January the Tsar danced with her and sat next to her at supper. She attended a huge number of balls, and she evidently enjoyed them so much that Pushkin was, at least sometimes, able to share in her enjoyment. According to a letter written by Sofya Karamzina at the end of January:

> Pushkin was very much afraid of malicious jokes about his appointment, but he has now calmed down. He goes to balls and takes pleasure in his wife's triumphant beauty. She herself, in spite of her dazzling successes in society, often and entirely sincerely suffers from jealousy – because the average beauty and average intelligence of other women do not cease to turn her husband's poetic head.

A great deal has been written about Pushkin as victim. The difficulties of his last years, and his eventual death, have been blamed on the Tsar or – more generally – on court intrigues. This view is too simple. The relationship between Pushkin and the Tsar was complex, and it certainly included mutual respect and affection. As for this humiliating appointment, Pushkin was probably being sincere when he wrote two months later to Nashchokin, 'Of course, in making me a *kammerjunker*, the Sovereign was thinking not of my age but of my rank – and he certainly did not intend to wound me.' Nicholas' greatest failing – at least with regard to his treatment of Pushkin – stemmed from his being a pedant; like many monarchs before and since, he found it difficult to see the world except through the prism of rules, ranks and etiquette. This may not even have been a personal failing; the American Slavist Caryl Emerson has written, with regard to the Russian aristocracy's wholesale importing of Western culture, 'To the extent that the court society of Tsar Nicholas I had a "native language", it was protocol itself.'[16] From the Tsar's point of view, Pushkin's modest rank in the Civil Service seemed to make him eligible only for a junior appointment at court. Nicholas had at least some sense of Pushkin's greatness as a poet, but it may never have occurred to him that this might be considered enough to qualify Pushkin for the higher court appointment of *kammerger* or chamberlain – a title that, according to his friend Vyazemsky, Pushkin would have felt honoured by.

Even if Pushkin came to accept that the Tsar had not intended to humiliate him, court life still entailed a vast expense of both money and time. It increased his expenditure at the same time as depriving him of the time he needed in order to write – which was the only way he could have increased his income. And, as we have seen, Pushkin was afraid that he might look absurd beside his younger fellows. From now until his last days, his letters are peppered with sarcasms about his title and his uniform. In April 1834, for example, he wrote to Natalya, 'I found out from Zhukovsky, who dropped in on me, that the Sovereign has been displeased at the absence of so many chamberlains and *kammerjunkers* [...] They say that we are going to march in pairs, like schoolgirls.' And in June he wrote, also in a letter to Natalya, 'I went to Her Highness' [...] in that pleasant mood in which you are accustomed to see me when I put on my magnificent uniform.'

Nevertheless, regular meetings with the Tsar at court functions brought with them certain rewards and privileges. Pushkin had long admired the Empress, and he was glad to be presented to her. Nicholas himself often talked with Pushkin and seems to have taken a genuine interest in at least some of his work, certainly in his *History of Pugachov*. This emboldened Pushkin to ask, through Count Benckendorff, for a loan to cover publication costs; he asked for more money than he needed, hoping to pay off other debts. Nicholas agreed that Pushkin should receive an interest-free loan of 20,000 roubles. He asked for only a very few changes to the text; the most important was that the title be changed from *A History of Pugachov*, which he thought endowed the rebel leader with too much dignity, to *A History of the Pugachov Rebellion*.

Pushkin's relations with the Tsar might have continued to improve but for another crisis. On 20th April Pushkin wrote, in a letter to Natalya, with regard to the Grand Duke Alexander's forthcoming sixteenth birthday and attainment of his legal majority:

I have no intention of going to see the Heir, with congratulations and greetings; his reign is yet to come, and I shall probably not live to see it. I have seen three tsars: the first ordered my little cap to be taken off me and scolded my nurse on my account; the second was not gracious to me; although the third has been so good as to appoint me a *kammerpage* as I approach old age, I have no wish to exchange him for a fourth. Better let well alone. We'll see how our little Sasha gets on with his namesake born to the purple. I did not get along with mine. God grant that he do not follow in my footsteps, write verses and quarrel with tsars. Then he won't outshine his father in verses, but he'll understand that might is right.

Pushkin's letter is bitter but witty. The first of the three Tsars is Paul I. The second is Alexander I, who had sent Pushkin into exile. The third Tsar, Nicholas I, had, of course, appointed Pushkin a *kammerjunker* rather than a *kammerpage*, which was a rank given only to boys.

The letter was opened by the police, and Benckendorff forwarded it to the Tsar. Zhukovsky, fortunately, was able to pacify Nicholas, but Pushkin was furious about his letters being opened and seems to have remained furious for the next two months. On 18th May he wrote to his wife, 'If the post has unsealed a husband's letter to his wife, then that's its affair. The one unpleasant thing is that the privacy of family relationships is being intruded upon in a foul and dishonourable manner. [...] Without privacy there is no family life.' And on 3rd June he wrote:

> I haven't written to you because the swinishness of the post has so chilled me that I haven't had the strength to take a pen in hand. The thought that someone is eavesdropping on you and me is literally driving me mad. It's quite possible to live without political liberty; without family inviolability it's impossible: penal servitude is a lot better. It is not for you I am writing this.

Pushkin's fury seems to have made him more determined than ever to escape to the country. On 29th May he wrote to Natalya, somewhat moralistically:

> ... with your leave, it will be necessary, I'm afraid, for me to go into retirement and to lay aside with a sigh my *kammerjunker* court-dress uniform [...] You're young, but you're already the mother of a family, and I'm certain that it won't be more difficult for you to fulfil the duty of a good mother than it is for you now to fulfil the duty of an honest and good wife. Lack of independence and of order in one's domestic affairs is terrible in a household. And no successes of vanity can take the place of tranquillity and content.

On 8th June he wrote:

> I have never thought of reproaching you for my dependent state. [...] The dependency caused by family life makes a man more moral. The dependency that we impose on ourselves from ambition or from need lowers us. Now they

look on me as a flunkey, whom they may treat as they please. Disgrace is easier to bear than disdain.

And on 28th June he wrote:

I am wholly at fault towards you with regard to money. I had money… and I lost it at cards. But what could I do? I was so full of spleen that I had to amuse myself somehow. *He* is to blame for everything; but God be with him; if only he would let me retire to the country.

Three days before this last letter, however, Pushkin had written a strangely curt note to Benckendorff:

Since family affairs require my presence sometimes in Moscow, sometimes in the provinces, I see myself obliged to retire from the service and I beg Your Excellency to obtain for me permission for this.

I would ask, as a final favour, that the authorisation which His Majesty has deigned to grant me, that of visiting the archives, not be withdrawn from me.

Once again the Tsar discussed Pushkin's behaviour with Zhukovsky. Zhukovsky promptly wrote to Pushkin, expressing astonishment that Pushkin had not told him anything himself, and continuing:

I only asked: 'Is it impossible somehow to put this right?' 'Why should it be impossible?' the Tsar replied. 'I never detain anyone, and I shall allow him to retire. But in that case everything will be finished between us.'

The last phrase indicates that Pushkin would no longer be able to use the archives that were so important to him. What is striking about it, however, is that it sounds closer to the language of lovers than to the language one expects from a Tsar having to deal with a troublesome subject. Once again it seems as if Nicholas felt personally hurt by what he probably saw as Pushkin's ingratitude. After further exchanges of letters between Pushkin and Benckendorff, and between Pushkin and Zhukovsky, the incident blew over; Pushkin would remain a *kammerjunker*; he would remain in St Petersburg, and he would continue to enjoy access to state archives. Zhukovsky's second letter deserves quotation; as always when rescuing Pushkin from his faux pas, he did not mince his words:

I never imagined that there was still the possibility of remedying that which you were pleased so recklessly to spoil. If you do not avail yourself of this possibility, then you will be that bristly animal, which feeds on acorns and with its grunts offends the ears of every well brought-up gentleman; put plainly, you will be acting badly and stupidly, you will ruin yourself for your whole life and will deserve your own and your friends' disapprobation.[17]

Pushkin's clear and honest reply indicates the depth of the unhappiness into which he was sinking:

I submitted my resignation in a moment of spleen and vexation at everybody and everything. My domestic circumstances are difficult. My position is not a cheering one. A change in my way of life is almost a necessity. I lacked the courage to explain all this to Count Benckendorff. This must have made my letter seem dry; really, it was simply stupid.

The next twelve months passed by without crises, but with no improvement in Pushkin's situation. In late June 1834 he wrote to his old friend, Praskovya Osipova,

There is no doubt that Boldino deserves to be saved, if only for Olga and Lev, who face the prospect of beggary or, at the very least, poverty. But I am not rich. I have a family of my own dependent on me, and which without me will fall into destitution. I have taken on an estate that will bring me only anxieties and unpleasantnesses. My parents do not know that they are on the verge of total ruin.

In July, Natalya persuaded him, against his wishes, to allow her two sisters to come and live with them in their St Petersburg apartment; she was hoping to sponsor them in society and so help them find husbands. Not long after this he wrote to her, with an uncharacteristic sourness, 'What kind of helpers or workers are the lot of you? You work only with your little feet at balls, and you help your husbands to squander.'

In September 1834, Pushkin again spent two weeks in Boldino. He needed to attend to the management of the estate, but he was also hoping – as he wrote to Natalya – that he might 'get into a writing vein'. In the event he wrote 'The Tale of the Golden Cockerel'; this 'fairy tale' about the relationship between a wise man and a tsar clearly hints at some of Pushkin's own resentments towards Nicholas. Pushkin also, in the same letter to his wife, mentions reading Walter Scott and the Bible. The Bible, and the Gospels, were growing more and more important to Pushkin during his last years. Pyotr Vyazemsky's son wrote in a memoir that Pushkin repeatedly urged him to spend more time reading both the New and the Old Testaments, and Pyotr Vyazemsky himself wrote shortly after Pushkin's death that Pushkin 'loved to read the Gospels, was deeply moved by the beauty of many prayers, knew them by heart and often repeated them'.

The History of the Pugachov Rebellion was published in late November. It attracted little attention. Pushkin's popularity with the reading public had by then been waning for some years, and his *History* was probably too unusual, too unlike any other historical writing of the time. When Pushkin died, over half of the 3,000 copies he had had printed were still unsold. Instead of making money as he had hoped, Pushkin lost around 4,000 roubles.

In July 1835 Pushkin made one last attempt to set his life in order. It was clear that no one but the Tsar could give him the help he needed. He drafted a letter asking for a loan of 100,000 roubles; this would enable him to pay all his debts, arrange his family's affairs and be 'at last free to abandon myself without worries to my historical works'. Having decided not to send this, he wrote a carefully phrased request to be granted leave to retire to the country for three or four years. The Tsar replied that Pushkin was free to resign, but that it was impossible to grant him leave for such a long period. Pushkin did not want to resign, since this would have meant losing access to the archives. After several more exchanges of letters, the Tsar agreed to allow Pushkin four months' leave and an interest-free loan of 30,000 roubles. This may have been generous, but not generous enough to make a real difference to Pushkin's situation.

The last years of Pushkin's life seem like an unending series of defeats, frustrations and sorrows. Once again, though, we see a different picture if we focus not on the life but on the work. As well as being a great poet, playwright and prose-writer, Pushkin was also a great journal editor. In the four issues of *The Contemporary* that he edited during his last year, Pushkin published a remarkable amount of great literature.

Pushkin had dreamed of editing a journal since his early twenties. Throughout most of 1830 he had helped Delvig to edit *The Literary Gazette*. In June 1831 he had written to the Tsar asking permission to found a newspaper 'that would be of service to the government', but he had then lost interest in the project, realising that it would leave him with no time for work of his own.

In late December 1835 Pushkin wrote to Benckendorff, saying, 'I would like during the next year, 1836, to publish four volumes of purely literary articles (also stories, poems, etc.), historical and scholarly articles, and also of critical analyses of Russian and foreign literature; similar to the English quarterly reviews.' Pushkin hoped that this journal would prove to be a way of making money. He probably also hoped to introduce a greater degree of professionalism into the Russian literary world.

The Tsar gave his permission, and the first 320-page issue of *The Contemporary* came out on 17th April 1836. This first issue was remarkable not only for including two stories by the still little-known Nikolai Gogol but also for the poem on its first page: Pushkin's 'Feast of Peter the Great'. This is written in a light ballad-like metre, but it is more serious than it first seems. The first four stanzas ask why celebrations are being held throughout St Petersburg. Because of some military victory? Because it is the anniversary of Poltava? Because his wife has given birth? Because it is her name-day? In the fifth and final stanza the speaker explains that Peter is celebrating because he is making peace with one of his subjects: 'he is celebrating forgiveness, like a victory over an enemy.' Once again, as in his 1826 poem 'Stanzas', Pushkin is exhorting the Tsar to forgive the exiled Decembrists; it would soon be the tenth anniversary of the execution of the five leaders.

The fourth issue of *The Contemporary* – the last to appear in Pushkin's lifetime – would include not only *The Captain's Daughter* and an article by Pushkin about the eighteenth-century Russian scientist and polymath Mikhail Lomonosov, but also twenty-seven poems by Fyodor Tyutchev. This was the first major publication of the work of the Russian poet commonly seen as second only to Pushkin.

For all its quality, however, *The Contemporary* had only 790 subscribers. On the one hand, Pushkin had enemies in high places; on the other, younger writers in Moscow saw him as an old-fashioned aristocrat and had begun to ignore him. Binyon calculates that Pushkin lost 10,000 roubles through *The Contemporary*, in addition to the 15,000 roubles he could have earned from publishing *The Captain's Daughter* and other works elsewhere.

Duel
1836–7

… To owe
Account to no one, serve oneself alone,
And please oneself, and breathe without delivering
One's conscience, thoughts or neck to power or livery…

Pushkin, 'From Pindemonte', 1836, tr. Antony Wood

Pushkin was growing ever more deeply depressed and more easily angered. In the autumn of 1835 he had publicly lampooned Dmitry Uvarov, the Minister of Education; he was angry with Uvarov because he considered him to blame for the poor reception of *Pugachov*. Even if this was the case – and it may not have been – Pushkin gained nothing from making Uvarov into even more of an enemy than he had been before.

In February 1836 Pushkin issued two challenges to duels, and he nearly issued a third. Fortunately none of these led to anything. One of the men Pushkin challenged was Count Vladimir Sollogub; Pushkin had heard a false rumour according to which Sollogub had insulted Natalya. Sollogub describes calling on Pushkin early in the morning: 'He came out to me in a dressing gown, still half asleep, and began to clean his extraordinarily long nails.' After discussing who were to be their seconds, they talked a little about *The Contemporary*. '"The first number was too good," Pushkin remarked. "I will make the second more boring: one mustn't pamper the public."' When Pushkin's second, Nashchokin, appeared, looking equally sleepy, Sollogub realised that a duel would be absurd: 'looking at his peaceable countenance, I involuntarily came to the conclusion that not one of us wanted a bloody denouement, and that the point was how we were all to extricate ourselves from this stupid situation without losing our dignity.' They succeeded in doing this, and the two men ended up closer friends than before.

Other problems, however, were less easily resolved. Pushkin's debts were increasing; at the beginning of 1836 they amounted to at least 80,000 roubles. No less troubling were the rumours that Baron Georges d'Anthès, a French royalist exile and – from January 1836 – a lieutenant in the elite Chevalier Guards, was having an affair with Natalya.

Another source of grief was the death, on 29th March (Easter Sunday) of Pushkin's mother, Nadezhda Osipovna; she had been ill since October 1834, probably with cancer of the liver. Pushkin accompanied her body to the Svyatogorsk monastery near Mikhailovskoye, and she was buried near the graves of her parents, Osip and Maria Gannibal. While he was there, Pushkin reserved a plot of land for himself, next to his mother's grave.

The story of Pushkin's fatal duel has always generated intense feeling, extreme views and conflicting accounts. A vast amount has been written about many of the smallest details of the story, but there are important questions to which we have no answers. We know little about what the Tsar thought, or what he said to Pushkin during two important conversations. We know little about what Natalya felt during these months. We have a large number of letters from d'Anthès, but no sure way of knowing how much of them to believe. Zhukovsky's testimony is more reliable than most people's, but he was sometimes naïve.

D'Anthès was a handsome young man with unusual charm and a romantic aura; he had come to Russia in October 1833, in the company of the Dutch ambassador, Baron van Heeckeren, and had quickly been accepted by high society. The relationship between d'Anthès and van Heeckeren was extremely close. Van Heeckeren was probably homosexual; it is conceivable that d'Anthès was bisexual, but there is no clear evidence for this. During a year spent in the Netherlands from May 1835 van Heeckeren had tried to adopt d'Anthès legally. He had been unable to do this because he had not reached the legally required age of forty-five; his lawyer, however, had put in place a legal construction that was, to all intents and purposes, the equivalent of adoption.

By autumn 1835 d'Anthès had got to know Natalya and her sisters. In January 1836 he had written to van Heeckeren that he was in love with Natalya, and that she loved him. This was probably an exaggeration; it seems more likely that she liked him and was flattered, even excited, by his attentions.

In February 1836 d'Anthès tried unsuccessfully to seduce Natalya. According to one of his letters to van Heeckeren, she told him that she could offer him 'no more than her heart, because the rest does not belong to her'. Binyon doubts the truth of this, writing that d'Anthès' subsequent behaviour 'is the behaviour of a rejected lover, whose passion is not returned, rather than that of one secure in the love of his mistress, and only prevented by her virtue from enjoying her favours to the full'.[18] Van Heeckeren, either jealous or afraid of scandal, seems to have begged d'Anthès to break off the relationship. In two letters sent to van Heeckeren during the following month, d'Anthès writes as if it is he, rather than Natalya, who has decided to terminate the relationship. On 6th March he wrote:

... and God is my witness that since I received your letter I have decided to sacrifice this woman for you. It is a big decision, but your letter was so good, full of so much truth and such tender friendship that not for a moment did I hesitate [...] I have been avoiding her with the same care with which I earlier sought to meet her, I have spoken to her with all the indifference I could summon, but I believe that had I not learned all you wrote to me by heart, I would have lacked the will... [19]

During the next few months d'Anthès seems to have kept his word and to have avoided houses where he was likely to meet Natalya.

In July – in a rare extant letter – Natalya wrote to her brother, who was in charge of the Goncharov family estate, begging him to grant her an allowance equal to that of her sisters:

I openly confess to you that there are days when I do not know how to carry on the household, my head spins. I very much do not want to disturb my husband with all my little domestic troubles. I already see how sad and depressed he is, cannot sleep at night, and, consequently, in such a state is not able to work to provide us with the means for existence: in order to work his head must be free.

Binyon comments:

This hardly seems the letter of a woman interested in nothing but her fashionable toilette and her social success; nor of one who would have been seduced by the attractions of a d'Anthès.[20]

On 31st July, however, at a grand fête in Tsarskoye Selo, d'Anthès saw Natalya again. From then on he gradually began sending her notes and theatre tickets and seeking her out at social events. In what seems to have been an attempt to divert attention from this, he began to court her sister Yekaterina.

On 15th or 16th September d'Anthès wrote to Natalya, begging her to leave Pushkin and go away with him. Natalya responded by telling him not to come to their apartment again.

The 19th of October was the twenty-fifth anniversary of the official opening of the Lycée. At the annual reunion of his fellow classmates, Pushkin stood up to read a poem he had composed. While reading the first lines about the more carefree reunions of their youth, he broke down in tears, unable to go on. Five years earlier, he had composed a poem for the reunion of 1831, the year of the unexpected death of Anton Delvig. After a stanza about there being now six empty places, six friends already 'sleeping in the earth', he had gone on to say:

> It seems it will be my turn next.
> I hear dear Delvig calling me;
> The comrade of my lively youth,
> The comrade of my gloomy youth,
> The comrade of my youthful songs,
> Of feasts and of pure meditations,
> The genius who has gone for ever
> Calls me to join this throng of shades.

On 2nd November, Natalya's second cousin, Idaliya Poletika, invited Natalya to her apartment. Idaliya had once been fond of Pushkin but had grown to hate him. Natalya arrived and was shown into the drawing room. There she found not Idaliya, but d'Anthès. He took out a pistol and threatened to shoot himself if she did not yield to him. Natalya was saved by the unexpected appearance of Idaliya's four-year-old daughter. Natalya did not tell Pushkin what had happened.

On 4th November Pushkin received an anonymous letter in French. He assumed that it was from van Heeckeren – but it would have been unlike van Heeckeren to go out of his way to create a scandal. The letter, copies of which were sent to a number of Pushkin's closest friends, stated that the members of 'The Most Serene Order of Cuckolds [...] under the presidency of the venerable Grand Master of the Order, His Excellency D.L. Naryshkin, <u>have unanimously elected Mr Alexander</u>

Pushkin to be deputy Grand Master of the Order of Cuckolds and Historian Laureate of the Order.' The last words of this letter are carefully chosen; they allude simultaneously to Pushkin's official position as 'Historian Laureate' and to the fact that the time when Pushkin himself used to seduce other men's wives was now over.

Most of Pushkin's friends destroyed their copies of this letter without opening it, suspecting that it contained some insult to Pushkin; the letter was in two envelopes, the outer one bearing the name of the friend in question, the inner one bearing Pushkin's name. Sollogub immediately called on Pushkin. On being shown the envelope, Pushkin asked Sollogub not to say a word about it to anyone: 'It is a vile slander against my wife. Though it's like getting shit on one's hands. It's unpleasant – but you wash your hands and that's the end of it.'

After Sollogub left, Pushkin spoke to Natalya. According to Vyazemsky, she told him everything that had happened between her and d'Anthès – and Pushkin did not doubt her innocence. Immediately after this conversation, Pushkin sent d'Anthès a challenge to a duel. Pushkin's letter was opened by van Heeckeren. He accepted the challenge on d'Anthès' behalf but begged Pushkin first for a day's grace, then for a week's. Pushkin granted him a fortnight.

Pushkin then seems to have given more thought to the details of the anonymous letter. The wife of Naryshkin – the 'Grand Master of the Order of Cuckolds' – had been the mistress of Alexander I. Pushkin may have seen the use of Naryshkin's name as a hint that Natalya was thought to be the mistress of Tsar Nicholas. Ever since their first meeting in 1831, Nicholas had singled her out at court. Natalya had flirted with him – as, no doubt, would most twenty-year-old girls who had attracted the Tsar's notice. It is probable that Pushkin trusted Natalya in this respect. He had, however, received two considerable loans from the Tsar in the previous two years – 20,000 roubles to pay for the publication of *Pugachov*, and 30,000 roubles in September

1835 to pay off his debts. Perhaps afraid that these loans might be seen as payment for his wife's services, Pushkin wrote to the finance minister, offering to pay back these debts – through a complicated and entirely impractical scheme. It was, of course, impossible for Pushkin to find such a sum.

On 7th November, Zhukovsky, trying to mediate on Pushkin's behalf, called on van Heeckeren. Van Heeckeren told him that d'Anthès was in love not with Natalya, but with her sister Yekaterina – and that he wished to marry her. Zhukovsky, taking this at face value, went to inform Pushkin – and was surprised by Pushkin's fury. Pushkin saw the marriage proposal as a sham and refused to withdraw his challenge.

Zhukovsky, van Heeckeren and Natalya's aunt, Yekaterina Zagryazhskaya, all tried to mediate. Zhukovsky was on the point of giving up when Pushkin finally, and reluctantly, withdrew his challenge. This may have been in response to van Heeckeren saying that d'Anthès had already seduced Yekaterina and that their marriage was therefore the only honourable way to proceed; there is evidence that Yekaterina truly was pregnant.

Several days later, d'Anthès seems to have realised that society would see his marriage proposal for what it was: a way of avoiding a duel. Pushkin had himself implied this. D'Anthès wrote to Pushkin, accusing *him* of dishonourably avoiding a duel. Pushkin asked Vladimir Sollogub – by then a good friend – to act as his second and to call on D'Anthès' second, d'Archiac, in order to arrange the conditions for a duel. Sollogub and d'Archiac managed to persuade both parties to climb down. On the evening of 17th November Pushkin congratulated Yekaterina on her engagement.

The public announcement of this engagement caused general astonishment. Few people believed that d'Anthès was truly in love with Yekaterina. Eventually van Heeckeren fell back on a different explanation: that d'Anthès had sacrificed himself for the sake of Natalya's honour. This view was to gain some degree of general credence, at least for the next few months.

D'Anthès then acted the role of the happy fiancé. Yekaterina, who may have been unusually naive or blind, seems to have felt genuinely happy. Pushkin continued to refuse to have anything to do with d'Anthès. Natalya seems to have felt anxious and confused. Wanting to stay close to her sister, she may have hoped to bring about a rapprochement between the two men. At the same time, she was probably afraid of enraging Pushkin; for some weeks he had been insisting that he would not even allow her to attend the wedding.

Pushkin did not calm down. On 21st November he wrote an insulting letter to van Heeckeren and read his draft out to Sollogub. Sollogub spoke to Zhukovsky. Zhukovsky persuaded Pushkin not to send the letter, telling him that he now considered it his duty to inform the Tsar.

On 23rd November Nicholas summoned Pushkin to an audience. There is no first-hand record of this conversation, but it is likely that Nicholas made Pushkin give his word never to engage in a duel. This meeting was followed by a period of relative calm.

Pushkin's main concerns during the next month were his debts and negotiations with publishers over new editions of his work. He also did a considerable amount of work for *The Contemporary,* both writing articles himself and soliciting contributions from others. The fourth issue of *The Contemporary* was published on 22nd December. This, as we have seen, included Pushkin's historical novel, *The Captain's Daughter.* Pushkin had completed a first draft in October 1835, but he had gone on revising it throughout most of 1836 and many of the concerns of his last year are reflected in it. The theme of honour is central; the book's epigraph is 'Take care of your honour when you are young.' In the last chapters, Masha, the bold, clear-headed young heroine succeeds, by petitioning the Empress, in saving the life of her fiancé; Sinyavsky has suggested that this reflects Pushkin's own longing for a wife who could save him.

For two weeks from 13th December d'Anthès was in bed with a chest complaint. When he reappeared in society, Pushkin seemed as furiously irritable as ever. D'Anthès and Yekaterina married on 10th January. Natalya attended the two ceremonies – one in St Isaac's Cathedral, one in the Catholic church of St Catherine; Pushkin himself attended neither. During the next few days van Heeckeren tried several times to bring about a reconciliation between the two men; Pushkin was unyielding.

On the evening of 23rd January Pushkin and Natalya attended one of the most important balls of the winter. Pushkin spoke again with the Tsar. Some years later, the Tsar talked about this conversation to Baron Korff, a historian and former fellow student of Pushkin's at the Lycée. According to Korff, Pushkin thanked the Tsar for some good counsel he had given his wife. The Tsar replied, 'But could you have expected anything else from me?' To this Pushkin responded, 'Not only could – but, to be honest, I suspected you too of paying court to my wife.'

Pushkin was still more enraged by d'Anthès, who not only flirted and danced with Natalya but also made a vulgar joke that was overheard by several people. The following day, Pushkin talked with Natalya; a young man who called in the afternoon found Pushkin sitting on a chair and Natalya sitting on a bearskin on the floor, her head on Pushkin's lap. From this point, having decided to act, Pushkin evidently felt a great deal calmer.

On the morning of 25th January Pushkin revised the letter to van Heeckeren that he had drafted two months before. This time he sent the letter; in it he referred to d'Anthès' cowardice, servility and despicable conduct, and he called van Heeckeren the 'pimp' of his 'bastard'. The following day, as Pushkin intended, d'Anthès challenged him to a duel.

It was difficult for Pushkin to find a second. Sollogub and his other friends were likely to try to bring about a reconciliation, or to inform Zhukovsky – who would inform the Tsar. And however the duel ended, the seconds would have been party to a criminal act. Pushkin began by asking an Englishman, Arthur Magenis; as a diplomat, he would have been immune to prosecution. After speaking to d'Archiac, d'Anthès' second, Magenis refused.

On the morning of 27th January, Pushkin received an impatient message from d'Archiac: he hoped to meet Pushkin's second 'with the shortest possible delay'. Pushkin responded by offering to accept as his second whomever d'Anthès chose, even if it were only one of his servants. In this Pushkin's behaviour was oddly like that of Onegin, who arrived an hour late for his duel with Lensky and appalled Lensky's second, the pedantic Zaretsky, by bringing a valet as his own second. D'Archiac said that the duel would be called off unless Pushkin provided a second in the normal way. In the early afternoon Pushkin found a second – Konstantin Danzas, an unmarried lieutenant-colonel who had once been a classmate of Pushkin's at the Lycée.

Back in his apartment Pushkin attended to *The Contemporary*. He wrote a letter to a woman who was translating some pieces by Barry Cornwall for it: 'I assure you that you will translate them in the best possible way. Today I chanced to open your *History in Tales* [Russian history retold for children], and involuntarily became engrossed. That's it – that's the way one should write!' This is a remarkable last letter – simple, generous, unpremeditated, yet indicative of Pushkin's deepest aspirations. His last published work, *The Captain's Daughter*, is subtle and complex, but it can be enjoyed by a child. It is easy to imagine Pushkin, had he lived, writing more 'history in tales'.

As Pushkin was writing this letter, Danzas and d'Archiac were agreeing to the conditions of the duel. These were unusual – calculated to bring about the death of at least one of the duellists; the barriers separating the two were to be only ten yards apart, even though the generally accepted code stipulated that the minimum distance should be fifteen yards. This was an 'advancing duel': the duellists were to start off about forty yards apart, advance towards each other on the command and fire at any moment after this command. Around three o'clock Danzas returned to Pushkin's apartment, and Pushkin at once agreed to the conditions. He then sent Danzas to Kurakin's 'emporium of martial objects' to collect the Lepage duelling pistols he had already chosen there. D'Anthès borrowed a pair of pistols from the son of the French ambassador, Ernest de Barante, who was later to use them in a (non-fatal) duel with the poet Mikhail Lermontov.

Around half past four Pushkin, d'Anthès and their seconds met at the prearranged spot on the outskirts of St Petersburg. Pushkin and d'Anthès were placed twenty yards apart and given their pistols. They began to walk towards each other. D'Anthès fired first. Pushkin fell to the ground, dropping his pistol. Saying he still felt strong enough to shoot, he asked for his second pistol. D'Anthès waited by the barrier. Raising himself up on one elbow and aiming carefully and accurately, Pushkin fired; d'Anthès fell. Pushkin asked where he was wounded. To d'Anthès' 'I think the ball's in my chest,' Pushkin replied, 'Bravo!'

D'Anthès' wound was only slight, but Pushkin's was serious. The bullet had passed through his abdominal cavity and shattered his sacrum; it was still lodged in the bone.

Pushkin was taken back home. Natalya collapsed. Pushkin was placed on a divan in his study. He repeatedly assured Natalya that she was not to blame for anything.

Danzas quickly brought several doctors, including Arendt, the Tsar's physician, to Pushkin's apartment. When Pushkin asked to be told the truth, Arendt said that he had almost no hope of his recovery. Spassky, the Pushkins' family doctor, suggested that Pushkin receive the sacraments; Pushkin at once agreed.

Pushkin's closest friends – Zhukovsky, Pyotr and Vera Vyazemsky, Alexander Turgenev, and Yekaterina Karamzina, the widow of the historian – all learned of the duel that evening. From then on at least one of them remained with Pushkin in his apartment. Zhukovsky from time to time put up a bulletin about Pushkin's health on the door to the street. The news had spread quickly and a crowd had gathered.

Arendt had conveyed to the Tsar Pushkin's plea for forgiveness. Nicholas replied with a pencilled letter to Pushkin granting him his forgiveness and telling him not to worry about his wife and children, saying that he would take them into his own care. This letter meant a great deal to Pushkin. According to Zhukovsky, he kissed it and said that he wanted to die with it. The Tsar, however, had already requested that the letter be returned; otherwise it would take on the force of an imperial edict.

In the small hours Pushkin's pain increased. Suspecting peritonitis and not knowing about his shattered sacrum, the doctors tried to give him an enema, causing Pushkin to scream. Princess Vyazemskaya and Natalya's sister, Alexandra, were sleeping in another room; his screams woke first them, then Natalya. This was the only such moment; Pushkin evidently tried to protect Natalya from knowing the extent of his pain.

During the morning, by then in somewhat less pain, Pushkin said goodbye to his children and to his friends. According to Princess Vyazemskaya, 'Each of his goodbyes was hurried, he was afraid of losing consciousness. Everyone who saw him left the room sobbing.' At midday Pushkin was given opium; why it was not given to him before is not known. Vladimir Dahl – the man who had once shown Pushkin around Orenburg and its environs, and who was later to compile the most renowned Russian dictionary – came to the apartment in the early afternoon and remained at Pushkin's bedside until the end. He had originally trained as a doctor, and it was he and Spassky who were to carry out the autopsy.

Pushkin remained concerned about Danzas. Through Arendt, he had asked the Tsar to show him leniency, but the Tsar had not mentioned him in his note. Zhukovsky decided to go to Nicholas himself; he asked Pushkin what he should say. Pushkin replied, 'Tell him it is a pity that I am dying. I would have been wholly his.'

As well as confirming a strength of feeling already evident from Pushkin's kissing of the Tsar's pencilled note, these words are oddly reminiscent of Nicholas' words about Pushkin at the end of their first meeting in September 1826: 'Now he's mine!' These two sentences effectively frame the relationship between Tsar and poet – a relationship in which there was probably deeper mutual affection than either was willing to admit. It is not impossible, however, that we owe this elegant structuring of their relationship to Zhukovsky's creative imagination. According to one account, Zhukovsky later confessed that Pushkin had never really said these words; he himself had made them up because he was 'concerned about the fate of Pushkin's wife and children'. Once again, the truth is elusive.

In the early afternoon of Thursday 29th January, after some hours of being barely conscious, Pushkin opened his eyes and asked for one of his favourite dishes: stewed cloudberries. When a plate was brought to him, he asked Natalya to feed them to him. She did this, kneeling beside the bed, and pressed her cheek to his. He then told Natalya to leave him.

Dahl has left the most complete record of Pushkin's last minutes:

> Squeezing my hand, he said, 'Come on, let's go, lift me up, let's go, higher, higher. Come on, let's go!' Coming back to himself, he said, 'I was dreaming that you and I were climbing up these books and shelves, high up, and my head began to spin.' Soon after this, without opening his eyes, Pushkin again took my hand, squeezed it and said, 'Come on, please, let's go – and together!'

Pushkin's last words of all were, 'Life is finished,' and then, 'It's hard to breathe. I'm suffocating.'

From Saturday morning until Sunday night a stream of people – over 10,000, according to Zhukovsky – came to the apartment to take their leave of Pushkin. It is hard to imagine so many people passing through the apartment in that time, but other people's estimates were higher still.

Afraid that they would be blamed for Pushkin's death and taken aback by the revelation of his popularity, the authorities then displayed extreme paranoia. University students and professors were forbidden to attend the funeral. The venue was changed without warning to a smaller church, and Pushkin's body was conveyed there late in the evening of the preceding day – not, as was usual, immediately before the service. Nevertheless, a huge crowd gathered in the square outside the church, rushing in when the doors were opened at the end of the service. According to Alexander Turgenev, 'the veneration for the memory of the poet [...] was so great that the front of his frock-coat was reduced to ribbons, and he lay there almost in his jacket alone; his side-whiskers and hair were carefully trimmed by his female admirers.'[21]

On the morning of 4th February, Turgenev set off with the coffin to the Svyatogorsk monastery near Mikhailovskoye where, after burying his mother the previous April, Pushkin had reserved a plot of land for himself. Twenty-six years before this, in 1811, it had been Turgenev who had enabled Pushkin to study at the Lycée. Natalya herself was in too hysterical a state to travel. Also accompanying Pushkin on his last journey was Nikita Kozlov, who had looked after Pushkin during part of his childhood and who had been Pushkin's valet ever since he left the Lycée. Kozlov sat on the cart beside the coffin all the way to Pskov. According to Turgenev, he did not move, eat or drink during the nineteen hours of the journey. It is hard, today, to imagine the intensity of feeling that may often have been present between master and older servant. Pushkin himself, however, has left us a moving portrayal of just such a relationship in *The Captain's Daughter*.

Turgenev arrived at Trigorskoye on the afternoon of 5th February, having left the coffin at a post station. Praskovya Osipova sent some of her serfs to the monastery to dig the grave.

Turgenev spent the evening with Praskovya and two of her daughters, talking about Pushkin. On 6th February Pushkin was buried.

Tsar Nicholas paid off all Pushkin's debts, and granted pensions to Natalya and the two daughters, and allowances to the two sons. He also arranged for the publication of Pushkin's collected works, with the proceeds going to Natalya and the children.

D'Anthès and his wife Yekaterina had four children, but Yekaterina died soon after the birth of the last of them, in 1843.

D'Anthès lived to the age of eighty-three; van Heeckeren to the age of ninety-two.

Natalya remarried in 1844, probably happily, and died in 1863, aged fifty-one.

'Exegi monumentum'

Not all of me shall die.

Pushkin, 'Exegi monumentum', 1836

The destruction of so great a genius as Pushkin, along with all that he might have gone on to create, is tragic. Not surprisingly, people have felt the need to find someone to blame. Soviet ideologues have, as we have seen, made out that Nicholas wanted Pushkin dead and that d'Anthès was 'a hireling of Tsarism'. Russia's two greatest women poets, Anna Akhmatova and Marina Tsvetaeva, are among the many people who have vilified Natalya. It seems to have been generally forgotten that she was an inexperienced woman in her early twenties, thrown almost without guidance into a situation of appalling complexity.

The need to find scapegoats is natural enough, but it is perhaps more fruitful to consider Pushkin's own role in the shaping of his fate. The defence of his and his wife's honour did not, after all, require him to fight a duel under such unusually dangerous conditions.

The idea that Pushkin was seeking death has some plausibility. As we have seen, he had issued three challenges to duels in early 1836. He was depressed and his mother had died recently. And the 'Stone Island' poems – an incomplete cycle of poems he wrote during this year – are very much concerned with death. 'When I leave the town and wander' contrasts a grotesque, crowded, city cemetery with a quiet, dignified, country graveyard like the one where Pushkin had just buried his mother and bought a plot for himself. And '*Exegi monumentum*', a re-working of Horace's claim to have built a lasting monument in verse, can be read as Pushkin taking stock of his achievements as he prepares himself for death. Its place among Pushkin's last works is all the more striking given that Gavrila Derzhavin had also written a poem with the same theme and title and that Pushkin's version is closer to Derzhavin's than to Horace's. Russia's greatest eighteenth-century poet gave his blessing to the brilliant fifteen-year-old at the Lycée – and his presence can be felt in one of Pushkin's last masterpieces. It was clearly Pushkin's aim, at this time, to impose an overall shape on his life's work.

Looking death in the face, however, is not the same as wishing to die – and there is nothing despairing about the strength and clarity of the 'Stone Island' poems. Yury Lotman has suggested that Pushkin can best be understood not as wishing to die but as exhibiting a supreme determination not to carry on living a worthless life. Lotman's argument has been summarised as follows:

> … in other words, Pushkin forced the use of the duelling code on the other side, knowing that *some change* (for example, exile to the country with his wife and family or death on his terms) would take place. And far from causing anxiety, this turning of his fate over to an artificial code gave him, for the first time in months, peace of mind and, possibly (had he lived), renewed *creative energy*. What Pushkin was willing to do was *gamble*, in the true spirit of gambling; what he was not willing to do was be the pitiful figure, the cuckolded husband in someone else's lowbrow comedy of manners.[22]

Pushkin was at his most creative when most tightly constrained. The constraints of the Onegin stanza enabled him to write with uncommon grace and fluency. Similarly, when he was in real danger – when he was 'in a tight corner' – he seems to have had a remarkable gift for saying the right thing. In everyday life he was often tactless and awkward, but during two crucial interviews – with Count Miloradovich in April 1820 and with Tsar Nicholas in September 1826 – he seems to have won his interlocutor's heart through the grace and charm he displayed while taking a courageous risk. At these two moments of crisis Pushkin gambled successfully. In *The Captain's Daughter*, incidentally, Pyotr Grinyov takes a similar – and equally successful – gamble by speaking boldly to Pugachov when they meet after the fall of Fort Belogorsk.

Pushkin's choice of Natalya Goncharova may itself have been a dangerous, but necessary, gamble. Caryl Emerson has written, 'Pushkin's creative nature sought steep and narrow walls within which it might rise. Without that pressure, perhaps his gift would have dissipated and lost focus. In choosing Natalya Nikolaevna, Pushkin chose unmanageable beauty, unmanageable debts, unprecedented vulnerability.'[23] The duel with d'Anthès may have been yet another, still more dangerous gamble.

If this is so, then the 'Stone Island' cycle can be read not only as a preparation for death, but also as a preparation for new life. In what may have been intended as the first poem, 'From Pindemonte', Pushkin tells us what freedoms and rights truly matter to him. The next three poems are a meditation, against the backdrop of Easter Week and its promise, on worldly power and spiritual power. In the fifth poem he asserts the superiority not only of country death over city death, but also – by implication – of country life over city life. And in *'Exegi monumentum'* he not only sums up his achievement, but also – in the last verse – reminds himself to be 'obedient to the will of God'. The future, at this point, seems more important to the poet than the past; what matters to him is to find a way of keeping his work fresh, alive and free of hubris.

Pushkin's oeuvre has a satisfying completeness as it stands, but every artistic conclusion is also, at least potentially, a new beginning. There is no knowing what Pushkin might not have achieved as a novelist, as an editor, as a historian – perhaps as a religious poet. *'Exegi monumentum'* was the final poem of Horace's third book of *Carmina*; Pushkin's version was probably the final poem of his 'Stone Island' cycle. To lead the reader back into the endless openness of Pushkin's work, I shall quote *'Exegi Monumentum'* in full, as translated by Antony Wood.

'Exegi monumentum'

I have built, though not in stone, a monument to myself;
The path that leads to it will not be overgrown;
Indomitably, the summit of my monument rises
　　Higher than Alexander's Column.

Not all of me shall die – for in my sacred lyre
My soul shall outlive my dust, it shall escape decay –
In the sublunary world my fame shall be unending
　　As long as a single poet holds sway.

And word of me shall spread through all the Russian lands,
My name shall be pronounced in all its living tongues,
By proud Slav race and Finn, by Kalmyk on the steppe,
　　And by the far-flung tribe of Tungus.

Long will there be a place for me in people's hearts,
Because in my harsh age I sang of Liberty,
Because my lyre awoke warm-hearted sentiments
　　And asked, for the fallen, Charity.

Be, O my Muse, obedient to the will of God,
To praise and calumny in equal measure cool,
Be not afraid of insult, seek no laurel-crown,
　　And do not argue with a fool.

Pushkin's legacy: my Pushkin or yours?

Pushkin is our all.

Apollon Grigoriev, 1854

The poet Apollon Grigoriev is no longer widely read, but his words about Pushkin struck a chord among Russians and have been quoted again and again. Not only is Pushkin Russia's greatest poet, he is also the author of the first major work in almost every literary genre. His position in Russian literature may be even more important than that of Goethe in Germany, of Dante in Italy or of Shakespeare in England. Once, in 1825, he referred to himself as the 'Minister of Foreign Affairs' on the Russian Parnassus. He was, of course, joking – part of the joke is that he was writing from exile and his family's remote wooden house in Mikhailovskoye was hardly the residence of a Foreign Minister – but Pushkin is often most serious when he appears most frivolous. He was at that time reading a great deal of foreign literature and responding to it through his own work, and it was his entirely conscious aim to make Russian literature into something of European importance. Like the Peter the Great he portrays in *The Bronze Horseman*, he wanted to 'break open a window into Europe'.

Pushkin's centrality to Russian culture has meant that not only writers, but also politicians, theologians and ideologues of all kinds have repeatedly battled to lay claim to his legacy.

Within a few days of Pushkin's burial an unknown 23-year-old Hussar lieutenant by the name of Mikhail Lermontov had won fame with his 'Death of a Poet', a fiercely rhetorical poem portraying Pushkin as a trusting Christ-like figure and accusing court circles of complicity in his murder. Lermontov was promptly exiled to the Caucasus, just as Pushkin had been exiled to southern Russia at a similar age. Both in his life and in his work, Lermontov continued to follow in Pushkin's footsteps, moving like him from Byronic Romanticism to a more classical, less subjective poetry and to prose that seems simple but is really very complex indeed; his *A Hero of Our Time* (1840) is the first great Russian prose novel. And like Pushkin, Lermontov was killed in a duel – at the still younger age of twenty-six.

Nikolai Gogol, with his love of the grotesque and of baroque exaggeration, is the most Rabelaisian of Russian writers. It would be easy to imagine him as deeply opposed to everything that Pushkin represents. Even Gogol, however, was keen to portray himself as a successor to Pushkin, claiming that Pushkin gave him the plots of both *Dead Souls* (1842) and *The Inspector General* (1836). The novelist and scholar Yury Druzhnikov has argued that this claim is one more of Gogol's vivid inventions. If he is right, then the strength of Gogol's need to invoke Pushkin's authority is all the more striking.

Lermontov died in 1841; Gogol lived until 1852 but published nothing of importance during his last ten years. The period immediately after Pushkin, Lermontov and Gogol was dominated by a group of earnest radical critics whose commitment was more to politics than to literature. The first of these, Vissarion Belinsky (1811–48), was respectful towards Pushkin. In 1838, only a year after Pushkin's death, he wrote, with a seriousness that might have made Pushkin uncomfortable, 'Every educated Russian must have a complete Pushkin, otherwise he has no right to be considered either educated or Russian.' Belinsky's successors, however, were often less respectful, and in the 1860s Dmitry Pisarev attacked the work of Pushkin – and poetry in general – for its uselessness. Dostoevsky satirised Pisarev's views in a sketch about a group of radical journalists whose central principle is that 'a pair of boots are, in every sense, better than Pushkin, because [. . .] Pushkin is mere luxury and nonsense [... and...] Shakespeare too is mere luxury and nonsense.' Several decades later, in 'What is Art?' (1898), Tolstoy would continue this line of thinking, dismissing Pushkin and Shakespeare – and most of his own earlier work – as frivolous. He also ridiculed the idea of making a national saint out of a dandy and womaniser like Pushkin.

In 1880 a now famous statue of Pushkin was unveiled in central Moscow. This was the first prominent monument to a literary figure in any Russian city and the celebrations lasted three days. Tolstoy had been invited to speak, but he had refused. Turgenev's relatively measured speech on the second day met with little response. On the final day, however, Dostoevsky gave his famous 'Pushkin Speech', claiming that the word of Christ is embodied, above all, in Russia and the Russian soul, and that 'the all-human and all-uniting Russian soul' is embodied, above all, in Pushkin. This very un-Pushkinian speech met with an ecstatic response and was a key moment in the process through which Pushkin was transformed into a national idol.

It is important to distinguish between Dostoevsky the novelist and Dostoevsky the Slavophile journalist and ideologue. Dostoevsky's journalism and public pronouncements were often – as on this occasion – crazily jingoistic. As a novelist, however, he has more in common with Pushkin than is at first apparent. Much of his greatness stems from his ability to give vivid expression to points of view opposed to his own; his socialists and atheists are as attractive, and come out with arguments as powerful, as the characters who express his own views. This enjoyment of polyphony is a gift Dostoevsky shares with Pushkin and that he could have learned from *The Little Tragedies* or *The Captain's Daughter*. The difference in scale between Pushkin's works and Dostoevsky's obscures some important similarities; as the example of 'Demons' (Pushkin's short poem and Dostoevsky's long novel) shows, there is a great deal of Pushkin in the swirl of Dostoevsky's novels – more, in fact, than in the more monophone novels of Tolstoy.

The centenary of Pushkin's birth in 1899 was celebrated throughout the nation and on a grand scale. The government did all it could to promote the image of a politically correct Pushkin, a Pushkin refashioned into a loyal defender of the autocracy. Streets were renamed after him, and schoolchildren were given free copies of his works and candy bars imprinted with his image. The range of Pushkin products on sale during the jubilee included 'Pushkin cigarettes, tobacco, rolling papers, matches, candy, steel pens, stationery, ink stands, liqueur, knives, watches, vases, cups, shoes, dresses, lamps, fans, per-fume ("Bouquet Pouchkine"), a variety of portraits and post-cards, plus a board game ("Pushkin's Duel").'[24]

The tastelessness of the board game was, not surprisingly, much criticised, but there is a certain superficiality about most responses to Pushkin during this period. A large number of operas were composed – ten of the twenty-two Russian operas inspired by Pushkin were written between 1880 and 1910 – but they are mostly more notable for their decorative 'Russianness' than for any serious engagement with Pushkin's texts. Rimsky Korsakov's opera-ballet *The Tale of the Golden Cockerel*, based on Pushkin's verse fairy tale, is typical in this respect. The 1914 Ballets Russes production in Paris was celebrated, above all, for its remarkable costumes and set designs. It is a curious foot-note to the story of Pushkin's relationship with his wife – who may well have been an unusually gifted dancer herself and who certainly enjoyed fine costumes – that these were the work of Natalya Goncharova, a great modernist artist who was a relative of Pushkin's wife and who was, in fact, named after her.

The years around the time of the Revolution saw a new serious-ness in attitudes towards Pushkin. In 1916 Andrey Bely published his first version of *Petersburg*, a novel set at the time of the 1905 Revolution and inspired by Pushkin at his most sombre; it is dominated by his Bronze Horseman – and the ring of his horse's hooves. In 1921, as we have seen, Vladimir Khodasevich spoke of a 'second eclipse of the Pushkinian sun'. And Alexander Blok, the greatest of the Russian Symbolists, said with similar gravity, during the same evening at the Petrograd 'House of Writers': 'It was not d'Anthès's bullet that killed Pushkin. He was killed by the absence of air. His culture died with him.'

The five greatest Russian poets of the first half of the twentieth century were all subjected to terrible political pres-sures. All turned to Pushkin for support, each invoking a differ-ent aspect of his life and work. Anna Akhmatova, whose own poetry was to grow increasingly cryptic over the years, wrote about Pushkin's talent for 'encryption'. Tsvetaeva, who always felt that she did not belong in this world, emphasised in her idiosyncratic 'My Pushkin' the ways in which Pushkin was an outsider – both because of his African blood and because every poet, in her view, is an outsider. Boris Pasternak, who survived the Stalin years partly because of his success in playing the role of a holy fool, wrote of 'the childlike Russian quality of Pushkin and Chekhov'. Osip Mandelstam, always intensely aware of the physiological sources of poetry, wrote, 'What makes Pushkin akin to the Italians? The lips work, a smile sets a line in motion, lips intelligently and merrily turn crimson, the tongue presses trustingly against the palate.' Even the Futurist Vladimir Mayakovsky eventually felt the need to appeal to Pushkin. In 1912 he had co-authored a manifesto titled 'A Slap in the face of Public Taste' and calling for Pushkin, Tolstoy and Dostoevsky to be 'thrown overboard from the steamship of modernity'. By 1926, however, he had realised that the battles he was fighting for the standing of poetry were only too similar to the battles that Pushkin had fought a hundred years before him. Behind Mayakovsky's 'A Conversation with a Tax Inspector about Poetry' stands Pushkin's 'A Conversation between a Bookseller and a Poet'.

Pushkin was equally important to poets, playwrights and prose writers, and to writers within and without the Soviet Union. Among Soviet writers, Andrei Platonov and Mikhail Bulgakov both wrote plays about him, and Platonov and Sigizmund Krzhizhanovsky both wrote important articles about him. Among émigrés, Vladimir Nabokov wrote what is still the most perceptive commentary to *Eugene Onegin*, as well as a strangely eccentric translation of it. Vasily Grossman is unusual among writers of this period in that he turned above all to the examples of Chekhov and Tolstoy, rather than to that of Pushkin; even he, however, wrote a dramatised version of Pushkin's unfinished novel *Dubrovsky*.

Throughout the Soviet period the battle for Pushkin's legacy continued. The State erected Pushkin monuments all over the Soviet Union and tried to co-opt Pushkin into the ranks of fighters for socialism; individual artists fought for their personal artistic visions – and for their personal visions of Pushkin. Many writers, including Tsvetaeva and Akhmatova, remained reverential towards Pushkin. Others, like the absurdist Daniil Kharms in the 1930s and Sinyavsky in the 1970s, were anything but reverential. Sinyavsky, in particular, emphasised the spirit of irreverent fun in Pushkin himself. A point of departure for Sinyavsky was the anonymous *anekdot* (joke or funny story) invoked on the first page of his *Strolls with Pushkin*:

And perhaps we will find it easier to get a sense of Pushkin if we approach him not from the front hall – with all its wreaths and its busts with a look of uncompromising nobility on their faces – but with the help of the anecdotes and caricatures sent back to the poet by the world of the street, as if in response to, or in revenge for, his resounding fame.

There were many such anecdotes about Pushkin – some absurd, some obscene, some politically subversive. In her introduction to her translation of Sinyavsky's book, Catharine Nepomnyashchy quotes one such anecdote told her by Sinyavsky himself:

Stalin is sitting in Heaven, and Pushkin comes to see him. 'Look,' he says, 'I had a girlfriend named Anna Kern. Can she be transferred to Heaven?' Stalin calls Beria [head of the secret police] and tells him, 'Kern has to be transferred to Heaven.' Beria answers, 'Well, you know, there's no room.' And Stalin says to him: 'But it's Pushkin who's asking!' 'All right,' Beria answers, 'I'll do it!' Pushkin comes to Stalin again and again and asks for more and more favours until finally Stalin in exasperation calls Beria and says, 'Ask d'Anthès to come here.'[25]

The humour is black. The Soviet cult of Pushkin reached its apogee in 1937, the year that marked both the centenary of his birth and the height of Stalin's purges. In February of that year a monument to Pushkin was unveiled on the site of his fatal duel; it was around the same time that Osip Mandelstam – amongst many others – was dying in the Gulag.

The ironies and absurdities of official Soviet culture are only too obvious. This makes it still more important to remember that, in spite of the political interference, a surprising amount of fine Pushkin scholarship was carried out in the Soviet Union. It was through discussion of Pushkin – more than of any other writer – that the great Formalist scholars of the 1920s (Yury Tynyanov, Roman Jacobson, Boris Eichenbaum and Viktor Shklovsky) developed their ideas. The 'Academy' edition of Pushkin's complete works (published 1937–59) has yet to be superseded. And Yury Lotman, the founder of Russian semiotics, published articles throughout his life on a huge variety of Pushkin-related topics: Pushkin and Dante, Pushkin and Robespierre, Pushkin and card games, Pushkin and duels... Russian semiotics is, in part, the product of Lotman's attempt to understand Pushkin.

One of the finest recent tributes to Pushkin is 'Sindbad the Sailor', a short story by Yury Buida, a writer who emerged during the 1990s. This three-page story is a moving evocation of madness; at the same time it incorporates material not far removed from that of the anonymous anecdotes about Pushkin and it reminds us how a poem, even when repeated in what may seem a mindless way, can still play a crucial role in someone's life.

The story's title, 'Sindbad the Sailor', is the nickname of a mad old woman who has lived on her own for the last twenty years. After her death, the town doctor and policeman enter her little house and discover that one room is filled almost entirely with sheets of paper:

All night long they sorted through the papers that Sindbad the Sailor had asked to be destroyed and which she'd hidden from sight for almost fifty years. Every day, starting on 11th November 1945, she'd written out one and the same poem by Pushkin: 'I loved you.' Eighteen thousand, two hundred and fifty-two pieces of paper of various sizes had been preserved, and those eight immortal lines were on every one of them, their beauty undimmed despite the lack of punctuation: the old woman had never used so much as a comma. She must have written from memory and had made many spelling mistakes; as for the word 'God', she'd always capitalised it, despite the Soviet orthography of the time.[26]

Madness is a central theme of the works Pushkin composed during his second 'Boldino Autumn'; it was something he feared deeply. The nature of his own religious beliefs is unclear, but he understood the meaning of prayer and he would have enjoyed this story about an old woman using a poem of his as a daily prayer, as a way of living with her madness. He might perhaps have felt it to be a confirmation of his claim that

> I have built, though not in stone, a monument to myself;
> The path that leads to it will not be overgrown...

Notes

1. Henceforth, all dates will be given only Old Style, i.e. according to the Julian calendar then used in Russia.

2. T.J. Binyon, *Pushkin* (HarperCollins, 2002), p. 66.

3. Binyon, *ibid.*, p. 177.

4. Binyon, *ibid.*, p. 223.

5. See Sergei Davydov, 'The Evolution of Pushkin's Political Thought' in *The Pushkin Handbook*, pp. 295–302.

6. My translation.

7. There is no happiness outside the usual paths.

8. All the bad omens.

9. V. Veresaev, *Pushkin v zhizni* (Sovetskii pisatel', 1936), p. 133.

10. Andrey Sinyavsky, *Progulki s Pushkinym* (Sankt-Peterburg: Vsemirnoe Slovo, 1993), pp. 69–70.

11. Catharine Nepomnyashchy, Introduction to Abram Tertz (Andrei Sinyavsky), *Strolls with Pushkin* (Yale University Press, 1993), p. 37.

12. Sinyavsky, *ibid.*, p. 7.

13. Alexander Pushkin, *Eugene Onegin*, tr. Vladimir Nabokov (Princeton University Press, 1990), p. 10.

14. Vladislav Khodasevich, 'Koleblemii trenozhnik', *Sobranie sochinenii*, ed. John Malmstad and Robert P. Hughes (Ann Arbor: Ardis, 1990), vol 2, p. 312.

15. Binyon, *ibid.*, pp. 478–9.

16. Caryl Emerson, 'Pushkin, Literary Criticism, and Creativity in Closed Places', in *New Literary History*, 29.4 (1998), p. 654.

17. Binyon, *ibid.*, p. 453.

18. Binyon, *ibid.*, p. 524.

19. Serena Vitale, *Pushkin's Button* (Fourth Estate, 2000), p. 63.

20. Binyon, *ibid.*, p. 539.

21. Binyon, *ibid.*, p. 634.

22. David Bethea, *Realizing Metaphors: Alexander Pushkin and the Life of the Poet* (University of Wisconsin Press, 1998), p. 132.

23. Emerson, *op. cit.*, p. 667.

24. Marcus C. Levitt, 'Pushkin in 1899' in *Cultural Mythologies of Russian Modernism*, ed. Boris Gasparov, Robert P. Hughes and Irina Paperno (University of California Press, 1992), pp. 183–204.

25. Sinyavsky, *Strolls with Pushkin*, p. 40.

26. tr. Oliver Ready, in Robert Chandler (ed.), *Russian Short Stories from Pushkin to Buida* (Penguin Classics, 2005), p. 377.

Chronology

1799 Alexander Pushkin is born on 26th May (6th June New Style)

1800–11 The Pushkin family live in Moscow; Pushkin is brought up mainly by governesses and tutors

1811–17 Pushkin studies at the prestigious Imperial Lyceum at Tsarskoye Selo, near St Petersburg

1812 Napoleon invades Russia, captures Moscow but then retreats, losing nearly all his army

1814 Russian and Prussian armies defeat the French outside Paris. Tsar Alexander I enters Paris in triumph

1815 Final defeat of Napoleon. Two of the greatest Russian poets of the time, Derzhavin and Zhukovsky, express their admiration of Pushkin

1816 Pushkin joins the innovative and irreverent literary society *Arzamas*. Death of Derzhavin

1817 Pushkin takes up a nominal appointment at the Foreign Ministry and begins a dissipated life in St Petersburg

1820 Pushkin is exiled to the south of Russia. Publication of *Ruslan and Lyudmila*. Travels with Raevskys to the Caucasus and to Crimea

1823 Pushkin, then living in Kishinev, starts work on *Eugene Onegin*. He is transferred to Odessa in July

1824 Death of Byron

1824–6 In August Pushkin is transferred to his mother's family estate at Mikhailovskoye, in the north

1825 Pushkin completes first version of *Boris Godunov*. Death of Alexander I. Decembrist uprising in support of a constitutional monarchy. Accession of Nicholas I

1826 Five of the Decembrist leaders are hanged; 120 Decembrists are exiled. In September Nicholas I pardons Pushkin and appoints himself his 'personal censor'

1828 Russia declares war against Turkey

1829 Pushkin travels to Transcaucasia and takes part in a skirmish against the Turks

1830 In the autumn, Pushkin is stranded in Boldino by a cholera outbreak. Writes *The Little Tragedies* and *The Tales of Belkin*

1831 Pushkin marries Natalya Goncharova on 18th February. Completes *Eugene Onegin* in August. Publishes *Boris Godunov*. Writes poems celebrating Russia's crushing of a rebellion in Poland. Is appointed 'Historian Laureate'

1833 Pushkin travels to Urals to research the Pugachov rebellion. Writes *The Bronze Horseman* and *The Queen of Spades* in Boldino

Bibliography

Pushkin in English

Boris Godunov: The Little Tragedies, tr. Stephen Mulrine
(Oberon Books, 2002)

The Captain's Daughter, tr. Robert & Elizabeth Chandler
(Hesperus Press, 2005)

Dubrovsky, tr. Robert Chandler (Hesperus Press, 2003)

Eugene Onegin – James Falen's translation (Oxford World Classics, 1995)
is better than any of its predecessors, but it is superseded by
Stanley Mitchell's new (2008) translation for Penguin Classics.
Mitchell's version is outstanding – a masterpiece itself

The Gypsies and other narrative poems, tr. Antony Wood (Angel Books, 2006)

The Letters of Alexander Pushkin, tr. J. Thomas Shaw (University
of Wisconsin Press, 1967)

Robert Chandler, *Russian Short Stories from Pushkin to Buida*
(Penguin Classics, 2005)

About Pushkin

David Bethea, *The Pushkin Handbook* (University of Wisconsin Press, 2005)

T.J. Binyon, *Pushkin* (HarperCollins, 2002). An authoritative, detailed
biography. I have been guided by it throughout

Chester Dunning *et al.*, *The Uncensored Boris Godunov* (University of
Wisconsin Press, 2006). This argues the case for the earlier version
of the play, which is included both in Russian and in Antony Wood's
translation. Much of what I say about the play is summarised from
Dunning's two articles

Elaine Feinstein, *Pushkin* (Orion, 1999)

Andrew Kahn (ed.), *The Cambridge Companion to Pushkin* (Cambridge
University Press, 2006)

Andrew Kahn (ed.), *Pushkin's Lyric Intelligence* (Oxford University Press,
2008)

D.S. Mirsky, *Pushkin* (Dutton, 1963)

Catharine Theimer Nepomnyashchy *et al.*, *Under the Sky of My Africa:
Alexander Pushkin and Blackness* (Northwestern University Press, 2007)

Yury Tynyanov, *Young Pushkin*, tr. Anna Kurkina Rush and Christopher
Rush (Angel Books, 2007). This novel by a famous Russian literary
critic closely follows historical sources

Serena Vitale, *Pushkin's Button* (Fourth Estate, 2000). This is florid,
but the information in it is reliable. Largely about Pushkin's last year

Acknowledgements

All passages from *Eugene Onegin* are quoted in the version by Stanley Mitchell; I am grateful to Penguin Classics for allowing this. I also thank Christopher Reid and Antony Wood for allowing me to quote from their versions of Pushkin's short poems, and I thank *The Independent* and *The Literary Encyclopedia* where earlier versions of some passages from this book first appeared. All unattributed translations (except from *Eugene Onegin*) are my own.

All dates are given Old Style.

There has not been room in this volume to include full references. Most important facts can be found in Binyon's biography, in Pushkin's own letters and in Veresaev's *Pushkin v zhizni*. I have also drawn on work by Hugh Barnes, Michael Basker (especially with regard to 'Arion'), David Bethea, Anthony Briggs, Sergei Davydov, Chester Dunning, Caryl Emerson, Jane Grayson, Catriona Kelly, Yury Lotman, Vladimir Nabokov, Catharine Nepomnyashchy and Andrey Sinyavsky.

Frans Suasso has been extraordinarily generous with his encyclopaedic knowledge of Pushkin. I also thank all of the following for their help: Michele Berdy, David Black, Elizabeth Chandler, Olive Classe, Sasha Dugdale, Carol Ermakova, Andrew Kahn, Elena Kolesnikova, Olga Meerson, Stanley Mitchell, David Powelstock and Antony Wood.

Biographical Note

Robert Chandler has translated the poetry of Sappho and Apollinaire. His translations from Russian include Vasily Grossman's *Life and Fate*, Pushkin's *Dubrovsky* and *The Captain's Daughter* and numerous works by Andrey Platonov. His translations have won prizes in both the UK and the USA. He teaches part time at Queen Mary College, University of London, and has published poems in the *TLS* and *Poetry Review*.